T0358226

Cambridge Elements

Elements in Ethics
edited by
Ben Eggleston
University of Kansas
Dale E. Miller
Old Dominion University, Virginia

EPISTEMOLOGY AND METHODOLOGY IN ETHICS

Tristram McPherson
The Ohio State University

CAMBRIDGE
UNIVERSITY PRESS

CAMBRIDGE
UNIVERSITY PRESS

University Printing House, Cambridge CB2 8BS, United Kingdom

One Liberty Plaza, 20th Floor, New York, NY 10006, USA

477 Williamstown Road, Port Melbourne, VIC 3207, Australia

314–321, 3rd Floor, Plot 3, Splendor Forum, Jasola District Centre, New Delhi – 110025, India

79 Anson Road, #06–04/06, Singapore 079906

Cambridge University Press is part of the University of Cambridge.

It furthers the University's mission by disseminating knowledge in the pursuit of education, learning, and research at the highest international levels of excellence.

www.cambridge.org
Information on this title: www.cambridge.org/9781108713405
DOI: 10.1017/9781108581493

First published 2020

A catalogue record for this publication is available from the British Library.

ISBN 978-1-108-71340-5 Paperback
ISSN 2516-4031 (online)
ISSN 2516-4023 (print)

Epistemology and Methodology in Ethics

Elements in Ethics

DOI: 10.1017/9781108581493
First published online: May 2020

Tristram McPherson
The Ohio State University

Author for correspondence: Tristram McPherson, dr.tristram@gmail.com

Abstract: This Element introduces several prominent themes in contemporary work on the epistemology and methodology of ethics. Topics addressed include skeptical challenges in ethics, epistemic arguments in metaethics, and what (if anything) is epistemically distinctive of the ethical. Also considered are methodological questions in ethics, including questions about which ethical concepts we should investigate, and what our goals should be in ethical inquiry.

Keywords: moral epistemology, methodology, ethics, moral skepticism, ethical knowledge

ISBNs: 9781108713405 (PB), 9781108581493 (OC)
ISSN: 2516-4031 (online), 2516-4023 (print)

Contents

1 Introduction

This Element aims to introduce you to a range of deep and abstract philosophical questions. The broadest of these questions can be illustrated by a concrete example from my own life.

When I was twenty, I went fishing with my dad. We took a rowboat onto beautiful Nicola Lake, caught some fish, took them back to my place, and cooked and ate them. I remember feeling uneasy throughout the process. I hadn't seen my parents for a few months, and was very glad for their visit. But as I would describe it later, I would have enjoyed sitting in a boat with my dad more if we weren't trying to drag animals into the boat in order to kill them. I found the killing of the fish viscerally unpleasant.

This, in turn, prompted further reflection. I realized that, while I had struggled to kill a fish, I would not be at all willing to kill a pig or a cow in order to eat it. I then thought something like, "if I am not willing to kill an animal in order to eat it, I shouldn't eat it."[1] In light of this reasoning, I became a vegetarian.

The aim of this anecdote is not to convert you to vegetarianism. Rather it is to provide a concrete example that we can use to identify and distinguish the sorts of questions that are the focus of this Element.

First, my reasoning was – at least in part – oriented around an *ethical* question: "Should I eat meat?" I at least implicitly drew the conclusion that I should not. If we ask whether my answer to this question was correct, or argue about this, we are engaged in ethics.

Second, we can ask *epistemic* questions about my conclusion that I shouldn't eat meat. For example, given how I came to this conclusion, we can ask: did I *understand* why I shouldn't eat meat? Did I *know* whether I should eat meat? Could anyone know something like that?

Third, we can ask *methodological* questions about the process by which I came to my conclusion. Was I addressing the right question in my reasoning? Given the question that I was addressing, was there a better way of reasoning about it? What would count as success in reasoning about such a question?

This short Element aims to introduce the reader to prominent themes in contemporary philosophical work on the epistemology and methodology of ethics. This introduction expands upon the very brief orientation to ethical, epistemic, and methodological questions just offered. It then briefly outlines the relationship between methodological and epistemic questions about ethics, and

---

[1] In this Element, terms in single quotation marks (e.g. 'skepticism') are used strictly to mention linguistic items. Double quotation marks (e.g. "cat") are used for a variety of tasks including quoting others' words, scare quotes, and mixes of use and mention. Terms in small caps (e.g. CAT) pick out concepts.

how these classes of questions relate to different parts of ethical inquiry. Finally, it previews the main topics to be discussed in the Element.

I introduced the idea of an ethical question with a single example that has played an important role in my life: "Should I eat meat?" However, ethical questions arise in all parts of our lives. We guide our own actions, form opinions of others, and elect political representatives partly on the basis of our ethical assessments. Should you keep a potentially hurtful secret? How should you react to your friend's homophobia or contempt for your political beliefs? Should your church give sanctuary to an undocumented immigrant facing deportation to a country where her life is threatened? Should the government do more to protect the health of its citizens, or get out of regulating health and medicine altogether? I will understand *ethical* questions as including a wide range of types of questions, including the following examples:

(1) Is it morally wrong to secretly read your spouse's text messages?
(2) Am I morally required to keep my promise to my editor to complete this Element?
(3) Is suffering always morally bad?
(4) Is utilitarianism the ultimate moral principle?
(5) Is polyamory morally permissible?
(6) Ought I go for a bike ride after work today?
(7) Do I have any reason to take up a new hobby?

What do these questions have in common? I take them to have three features, which together are distinctive of ethical questions. First, these questions are broadly *normative* as opposed to *descriptive*: the first question, for example, does not ask whether people *do* secretly read their spouses' texts, but rather seeks moral guidance concerning whether to do so. Second, ethical norms have a distinctive topic: roughly, the guidance and assessment of actions and motives. Third, the normativity at stake in ethics appears to be distinctively weighty or important. This can be illustrated by contrast with questions like:

(8) Would moving my bishop be a *good chess move*?
(9) Do the norms of my criminal organization require me to kill this guy?

These are also normative questions about possible actions. But the norms of chess strike most of us as less weighty than the sort of normativity at stake in the first seven questions. And even if career criminals should sometimes conform to the norms of their criminal organizations (e.g. to avoid getting killed), those norms themselves seem less normatively important than the ethical norms.

One important division within the class of ethical questions is between *moral* questions (for example, questions [1–5]) and *non-moral* questions (for example, questions [6–7]). I will understand ethics broadly to comprise both of these sorts of questions.[2] Notice that ethical questions can be extremely specific – like question (2) – or extremely general – like question (4).

Contrast the questions just discussed with the following questions:

(10) Am I *justified* in believing that tomorrow will be sunny?

(11) Do I *know* that my child is at school right now?

(12) Who here *understands* Leibniz's theory of monads?

(13) How strong is the *evidence* for human-caused climate change?

These questions are *epistemic*, as opposed to ethical. Like ethical questions, epistemic questions appear to be weighty normative questions. It is controversial how to characterize the contrast between epistemic and ethical questions in general. One common and natural idea is that epistemic questions concern the guidance and assessment of beliefs and believers, as opposed to actions and motives. But we can have ethical reasons to form or abandon certain beliefs. (Or at least: to *bring it about* that we form or abandon such beliefs.)[3] For example, that a belief is *racist* might be a good ethical reason to abandon it.[4] And certain sorts of motives are central elements of plausibly *epistemic* virtues such as openmindedness or intellectual conscientiousness.[5] Another common suggestion is that epistemic norms contrast with ethical norms in bearing a distinctive explanatory relationship to truth. Perhaps, for example, for something to be *evidence* for a claim is for it to make it more likely that the claim is true (in an admittedly tricky to clarify sense of "likely.") But there is no uncontroversial way to make precise the alleged distinctive connection between epistemic norms and truth. In light of this, I will follow the usual practice and rely on examples like questions (9)–(12) to

---

[2] This leaves open how to classify certain normative questions, such as questions about justice in political institutions. It is controversial whether such questions are ethical, and I won't take a stand on that here. It is worth noting, however, that if such questions are not ethical, many of the epistemological and methodological ideas discussed in this Element will have analogues in the political domain. For more detailed discussion of the varieties of normativity, see Baker (2018), Darwall (2018), and McPherson (2018a).

[3] For this distinction and its importance, see, for example, Kelly (2003).

[4] Complicating things further, some philosophers have recently argued that the ethical character of beliefs can have epistemic implications. See, for example, Fritz (2017) and Bolinger (2018). And others have shown that there are specifically epistemic ways in which individuals can wrong each other, and in which social arrangements can be unjust. See, for example, Fricker (2007).

[5] On the ethics of belief see Chignell (2018). On epistemic virtue, see Turri, Alfano, and Greco (2018).

orient us to the epistemic.[6] These questions deploy four central epistemic relations: justification, knowledge, understanding, and evidence. Epistemologists discuss many other relations, but for simplicity, this Element will focus on these four.

The epistemology of ethics addresses epistemic questions about ethical claims. Some such questions are extremely specific. For example, consider:

(14) When I was 20, did I know that it was wrong for me to eat meat?

Typically, however, epistemologists of ethics focus instead on general questions, such as:

(15) In virtue of what is an ethical belief epistemically justified?
(16) Can we have any ethical knowledge?

One central reason for interest in the epistemology of ethics is that ethical knowledge can appear more puzzling, more elusive, and less secure than knowledge of many other topics. Indeed, philosophers have mounted a range of apparently powerful arguments that entail that we cannot have ethical knowledge. Section 2: Asymmetrical Skepticism about Ethics introduces such skeptical arguments and explores the resources that anti-skeptics can use to reply to these arguments.

A second reason for interest in the epistemology of ethics is that answers to questions in the epistemology of ethics could help us to make progress in our inquiry in and about ethics. Consider first how the epistemology of ethics is relevant to *metaethical inquiry*. The project of metaethics is to explain how actual ethical thought and talk, and the distinctive subject matter of that thought and talk (if any), fits into reality (McPherson and Plunkett 2018: 3). To make this project clearer, consider simple versions of two metaethical views. First, consider *anti-realist expressivism*. To a first approximation, the expressivist claims that ethical sentences such as 'I ought to resist racism' semantically express psychological states that are broadly desire-like, where non-ethical sentences such as 'I am late for class' semantically express beliefs. For example, some expressivists think that 'Hooray to my resisting racism!' is a good initial paraphrase of 'I ought to resist racism.' The *anti-realist* expressivist claims that their account of ethical thought and talk is inconsistent with the idea that there are ethical facts and properties for ethical thought and talk to be about. To see why this is a natural thought, consider the suggested paraphrase for an ethical claim. It would be confused to ask what property 'hooray!' talk was about. Next,

---

[6] For useful historical background to epistemic evaluation and its variety, see the introduction to Alston (2005). One unhappy hypothesis is that "epistemic" functions in contemporary philosophy as a perniciously undefined technical term (Cohen 2016).

consider a simple form of *naturalistic realism*. According to this naturalistic realist, the thought that I ought to resist racism is an ordinary belief. Ethical thought and talk is distinctively about certain ethical properties and relations, such as the ought–relation. Finally, ethical properties and relations are a part of the natural world: they are of a kind, metaphysically speaking, with the sorts of properties discovered by the sciences.

The metaethicist has reason to be interested in the epistemology of ethics because informative metaethical theories tend to have implications for the epistemology of ethics (McPherson 2012: esp. §4). The (im)plausibility of these implications can in turn affect the credibility of a candidate metaethical theory. Section 3: Epistemic Considerations in Metaethics explores some of these connections.

Given this understanding of metaethics, the epistemology of ethics will often be *part* of the metaethical project. For example, epistemic relations are one way that ethical thoughts can fit into reality. However, this Element will discuss the relationship between the epistemology of ethics and (other parts of) metaethics. Because of this, in what follows I will stipulatively use 'metaethics' in a narrower way that *excludes* the epistemology of ethics.

Consider next the relationship between the epistemology of ethics and normative ethics. Normative ethics aims to answer ethical questions, such as questions (1)–(7) that were mentioned above. The normative ethicist has straightforward reason to be interested in the epistemology of ethics. This is because an informative epistemology of ethics will help us to see what sorts of evidence can support ethical claims, and the conditions under which answers to her ethical questions count as justified, known, or understood. It is natural for the normative ethicist to care about which answers to her questions have these properties.[7] If one is interested in the epistemology of ethics for these reasons, one will naturally be interested in ways in which the epistemology of ethics is different from the epistemology of other topics. Section 4: The Epistemic Character of Ethics surveys influential proposals about how ethics might be epistemologically distinctive.

This Element concerns the epistemology and *methodology* of ethics. Above, we saw examples of methodological questions about my youthful reasoning concerning eating meat. But again, methodologists tend to focus on more general questions. The broadest methodological question about ethics is: how (if at all) should we answer ethical questions, such as questions (1)–(7)?

While the epistemology and methodology of ethics are distinct, it is natural to think that they are closely related. For example, facts about what it would be to

---

[7] Parts of this paragraph and the last draw upon McPherson (2018b).

know, to be justified in believing, or to understand an ethical claim appear directly relevant to the methodological question of how to go about answering an ethical question. And the methodology of ethics bears very similar relations to metaethics and normative ethics as the epistemology of ethics does. On the one hand, one would expect metaethical theories to have implications for the methodology of ethics. On the other hand, the broad methodological question about ethics just mentioned is of obvious interest to the normative ethicist.

As I explain in Section 5: Methodology in Ethics Beyond Epistemology, there are several important methodological questions that are less clearly parallel to questions in the epistemology of ethics. Consider an example. Suppose that one of the skeptical hypotheses discussed in Section 2 was vindicated, entailing that ethical inquiry cannot give us epistemic goods like knowledge. Even given this striking limitation, we could still ask methodological questions about how to proceed in ethical inquiry. The bulk of Section 5 discusses two central types of methodological questions. The first are questions about the *conceptual ethics* of ethical inquiry: roughly, questions about what sorts of ethical concepts we should organize our ethical inquiry around. The second are questions about the *goals* of ethical inquiry: questions that concern what we should be trying to accomplish by engaging in ethical inquiry.

It is worth distinguishing these sorts of broad methodological questions from methodology understood as the attempt to find some specific *method* by which we could answer any ethical question. Clearly it would be both interesting and useful if there were such a method. I conclude Section 5 by briefly discussing the most prominent candidate method in ethics: the method of reflective equilibrium. I suggest that, unfortunately, where this proposed method is informative, it is also quite implausible.

Moral epistemology and methodology are receiving increasing philosophical attention. My aim in this Element is to enable the reader to see the forest, and not just the trees, in this burgeoning field. For those who want to dive deeper into particular questions raised in the text, I include references throughout to guide further reading.

2 Asymmetrical Skepticism about Ethics

Imagine turning to your favored news source and encountering a headline proclaiming that ethical theorists had discovered that abortion is morally permissible in the first trimester. Whatever your views about the ethics of abortion, you would likely take the headline as a sign of journalistic incompetence. Or imagine telling a friend that you are studying ethical knowledge. They might well look at you as if you had announced you were majoring in astrology. These examples suggest that there is something puzzling about the very idea of ethical knowledge. For suppose that it were obvious that we can have ethical knowledge. Then no one would find the idea of studying ethical knowledge baffling. And surely ethical discoveries would deserve reporting in reputable news sources. These examples might seem to be symptoms of a deep fact about ethics: our inability to have ethical knowledge. This section introduces what can be said for and against this sort of *skeptical* conclusion about ethics.

I begin by clarifying the sort of skeptical thesis that is the focus of this section (Section 2.1). I then survey six important strategies for arguing for this sort of skeptical conclusion about ethics (Section 2.2). Finally, I introduce several resources that can be used to reply to skeptical arguments in ethics (Section 2.3).

2.1 Introducing Asymmetrical Ethical Skepticism

This section does two things. First, it distinguishes the view that is the focus of this section – what I call *asymmetrical ethical skepticism* – from a variety of other worries about ethics. It then introduces an important general framework for regimenting arguments for this sort of skepticism.

The term 'skepticism' is sometimes used broadly, to encompass a range of ways in which a topic or practice might fall short of some expectation. For example, views are sometimes called "skeptical" because they entail that ethics fails to be in some sense objective, or because they entail that ethical facts lack distinctive practical significance. The influential *Pyrrhonian* skeptic advocates for *suspending judgment* concerning whether we have epistemic goods like knowledge or epistemic justification (e.g. Sinnott-Armstrong 2006). In this Element I will use 'skepticism' more narrowly. On this usage, skepticism about a topic is the thesis that some distinctive epistemic good (such as knowledge) is unavailable to us with respect to that topic.

Some contemporary discussions of skepticism are framed in *dialectical* terms: they discuss whether the "anti-skeptic" aims to "play defense" against the skeptic or instead to "play offense." There are at least two dimensions to this contrast. The first concerns what an anti-skeptical argument needs to achieve: playing offense requires showing that one *can* have knowledge (or whatever epistemic good is at stake). Playing defense, by contrast, requires only that one demonstrate the weakness of the relevant skeptic's argument. The second dimension concerns whether one needs to provide an argument that is compelling by the skeptic's own lights. To play "offense" in this sense is to provide an argument that the skeptic ought to recognize is compelling. To play "defense" is to provide a response to the skeptic that one can recognize as compelling, even if it fails to compel the skeptic.[8]

---

[8] The first contrast is suggested by Kelly (2005: 181–82). Pryor (2000: 517) draws the second contrast, calling it the contrast between the "ambitious" and the "modest" anti-skeptic.

It is a familiar theme in recent epistemology that successful offense in either of these senses can be hard to pull off (or even impossible), while successful defense often appears more attainable. Framing our epistemic discussion in terms of "offense" and "defense" is controversial, however. For this framing suggests that our central concern is somehow to score points in discourse with the ethical skeptic. Because of this, I will instead frame my discussion around the question of whether we can in fact have certain epistemic goods in ethics.

One could argue for ethical skepticism by claiming that it is a consequence of a more general skepticism. There are many influential arguments for very general forms of skepticism. Consider two examples. First, *regress* arguments claim that any search for epistemic justification inevitably triggers a vicious justificatory regress. According to this sort of argument, in order to be justified, a belief must be based upon another belief or beliefs which are justified. But these justifying beliefs in turn need to be justified by some further beliefs, triggering the regress. Second, *skeptical hypothesis* arguments claim that there are hypotheses we cannot rule out that are inconsistent with our having any knowledge. One such skeptical hypothesis was made famous by René Descartes. This is the hypothesis that any of our beliefs – and the apparent evidence for those beliefs – might have been produced by a powerful being bent on deceiving us (Descartes 1984: 15). In this section, I largely set aside such arguments for general skepticism: they are important, but I take them to belong in a discussion of general epistemology.[9]

This section focuses on examining arguments for *asymmetrical* skepticism about ethics: skeptical arguments that target ethical beliefs without generalizing to most of our non-ethical beliefs.[10] One reason to take asymmetrical skepticism seriously is provided by the idea that I used to frame this section: that ethical knowledge can appear distinctively puzzling. Many contemporary epistemologists think that it is a mistake to orient epistemology around engaging with the skeptic. However, even if this is true in general epistemology, our distinctive puzzlement about ethical knowledge might warrant systematic investigation of skepticism about ethics.

As I mentioned in Section 1, there are many epistemic relations. And we can imagine skeptical hypotheses targeting various of these: a very ambitious skeptic could deny that we can have *evidence* about ethics, for example. Another

---

[9] For an excellent introduction to general skepticism, see Klein (2015). The most important systematic discussion of ethical skepticism – Sinnott-Armstrong (2006) – includes substantial discussion of the application of general skeptical strategies to ethics.

[10] I take this terminology from Jones (2006), which is an excellent (if now slightly dated) introduction to moral epistemology.

might propose that we can have ethical knowledge, but not ethical understanding. There are also more possible ways of structuring skeptical arguments than I could hope to introduce here. (It is worth keeping in mind that many of the skeptical challenges that will be discussed in Section 2.2 could be developed in a variety of ways that are interestingly different from how I present them.)

To simplify discussion, this section focuses on a single framework for developing skeptical arguments. Within this framework, skeptical arguments aim to show that our epistemic justification for accepting ethical beliefs is defeated. To clarify this framework, the remainder of this section introduces and explains the relations of (adequate) epistemic justification and epistemic defeat.

Suppose that I offer you $1,000 to believe that I am not yet forty years old. In a sense, this would give you excellent justification for believing that I am not yet forty: you would get a cool grand! However, this offer arguably gives you no *evidence* whatsoever for this belief. Indeed, the offer might well be evidence that in fact I am over forty: otherwise, why wouldn't I save the money and just show you my ID? *Epistemic* justification is the sort of justification paradigmatically provided by evidence. We can say, then, that my offer would provide you with *practical* justification for believing (or coming to believe) that I am not yet forty, while perhaps indirectly providing epistemic justification for disbelieving it. The skeptical arguments introduced below focus on the sort of epistemic justification paradigmatically provided by evidence, and not the sort of practical justification paradigmatically provided by beneficial consequences. (While this sort of distinction is widely accepted, I have not explained what it consists in, or shown that it survives critical scrutiny. Recall the difficulty of characterizing the epistemic that was briefly mentioned in Section 1.)

We can have more or less epistemic justification for a given belief. For example, I heard in a song once that the sun is made of plasma (as opposed to being a solid or a gas). This may give me some justification for believing this claim, but it is pretty flimsy. If this claim is true, an astrophysicist presumably has much more justification for believing it than I do.

On a very influential picture, knowing that a claim is true requires that your epistemic justification for believing that claim is above some threshold of quantity and/or quality. Perhaps most astrophysicists are above that threshold with respect to the claim that the sun is made of plasma, and I am not. Call justification that meets or exceeds this threshold, whatever it is, *adequate* epistemic justification.

I will focus on skeptical views according to which we systematically lack adequate epistemic justification for ethical beliefs, at least once we are presented with certain skeptical arguments. This sort of skeptical view does not entail that we entirely lack justification for our ethical beliefs, or evidence for those beliefs, or understanding of ethical truths (unless understanding why a claim is true turns out to require adequate justification for believing it).

I will consider skeptical arguments that attempt to show that we lack adequate epistemic justification by offering purported *defeaters* for justification. A defeater is a piece of evidence that prevents some body of evidence that would otherwise provide adequate justification for believing a claim from doing so. It is useful to distinguish three sorts of defeaters (cf. Pollock and Cruz 1999: 196ff and Christensen 2010).

A *rebutting* defeater presents evidence against the truth of the claim that another body of evidence supports. For example, suppose that Ava tells me that it is going to rain today. Supposing that Ava is trustworthy, this testimony would ordinarily adequately justify me in believing that it is going to rain. Suppose next that Zula tells me that it is not going to rain today, and that Zula is also trustworthy. In this case, the evidence provided by Zula's testimony *rebuts* the evidence provided by Ava's testimony. We can provisionally think of rebutting defeaters with the metaphor of a balance scale. We can imagine putting evidence for and against a claim on opposite sides of a scale, such that we count as having adequate justification for believing it only if the weight of the justification for believing it is appropriately greater than the weight of evidence against it. On this metaphor, rebutting defeaters function by weighing against the truth of the relevant claim.

Undercutting defeaters work without providing evidence against the initially justified claim. Rather – to continue our balance scale metaphor – they function by preventing a piece of evidence from weighing in favour of a conclusion. For example, suppose that I enter a room and notice that the table looks red. This would ordinarily provide me with adequate justification for believing that the table is red. But then I read a sign that says: "Some of the lights in this building can change how objects appear to be colored." The sign itself does not provide me with any evidence concerning the color of the table. But it does defeat my justification for believing that the table is red provided by how the table looks. Once I know that the lighting could be misleading, I am no longer adequately epistemically justified in believing that the table is red based upon how it looks. It is plausible that even if the lighting in this room is in fact normal, and the table is in fact red, my knowledge of the defeater can prevent my accurate perception of the table from adequately justifying me in believing that the table is red.

Next consider a third – and more controversial – sort of defeat, which I will call *higher-order* defeat. To strain our balance scale metaphor, higher-order defeaters function by suggesting that we should not trust our balance scale to weigh properly. Consider an example. Suppose there were a drug that typically causes people to become highly unreliable at doing logic puzzles and unable to detect their mistakes. I know the drug has this effect, and have taken the drug. Then I start doing some logic puzzles. The puzzles seem easy to me, and in fact the drug has not affected me: I am reasoning well to the correct answers.[11] Nonetheless, it might seem that I should not believe the answers I have arrived at: arguably, the fact that I know I have taken the drug entails that I should not trust my own reasoning about the puzzles, and this prevents me from knowing the answers to those puzzles by my own reasoning.

This section has clarified the skeptical hypothesis that will be my focus: this is the thesis that we entirely lack adequate epistemically justified ethical beliefs, at least once presented with certain skeptical arguments. The section has also clarified the structure of those arguments, which involves purporting to identify *defeaters* for our justification for ethical beliefs. With this in place, we can now consider some important types of arguments for this sort of skepticism.

2.2 Arguing for Asymmetrical Skepticism: Six Strategies

This section seeks to briefly introduce six of the most influential bases on which one might argue for asymmetrical skepticism in ethics. These bases are:

- Distinctive features of the psychology of ethical beliefs
- The genesis of ethical beliefs
- The (alleged) lack of explanatory connection between ethical facts and ethical beliefs
- The prevalence and nature of ethical disagreement
- Epistemically unfriendly metaethical hypotheses
- Epistemically unfriendly metaphysical hypotheses.

In each case, I formulate a simple schematic skeptical argument that illustrates the skeptical strategy, and then briefly motivate and explore the skeptical worries that underlie the argument.

The first schematic argument appeals to facts about the psychological role of our ethical beliefs:

1. Our ethical beliefs and reasoning are sensitive to psychological pressures that often lead us away from the truth.
2. The fact mentioned in premise 1 defeats our existing justification for each of our ethical beliefs.

---

[11] Compare Christensen (2010: 187).

3. The only way to justify our ethical beliefs in the face of this defeater inevitably involves engaging in more ethical reasoning, which is subject to the same defeater.

4. So we lack justification for any of our ethical beliefs.[12]

Let me begin by explaining the structure of this argument. Premise 1 of the argument makes a claim about our ethical beliefs and reasoning (which I will discuss further below). Premise 2 claims that this claim about our ethical beliefs is a defeater for their justification, in the sense discussed in Section 2.1. Faced with such a defeater for one's belief, one might seek to find new justification for that belief that is unaffected by the defeater. (To see why one might seek such evidence, recall our initial example of an undercutting defeater involving unusual lighting: in light of this defeater, one might take the table outside into natural light to check its color. By doing so, one would be acquiring new evidence that is unaffected by the defeater.) However, premise 3 states that in the ethical case, any such attempt at novel confirmation is subject to the same defeater, so there is no escaping the defeat.

In support of the first premise, the skeptic can appeal to at least three sorts of apparent facts. First, we have a stake in which ethical claims are widely believed. For example, it would be to the advantage of some, and the disadvantage of others, if it was widely held that we have a strong duty to aid the needy, or that justice required reparations for slavery. And it is a familiar fact that such stakes can influence our beliefs about what is right or just. Second, our ethical beliefs are often intimately entangled with emotions like disgust, guilt, contempt, and resentment. Think, for example, of how common it is to have strong feelings about corrupt politicians or pedophiles. This raises the possibility that our ethical judgments are sometimes influenced by visceral emotional reactions. Third, many people appear to have a strong tendency to believe that they are good – or at least decent. In cases where we notice that we are not behaving decently, this can lead us to behave better. But it can also create pressure to change our ethical beliefs so that we perceive our own behavior – and that of our friends and loved ones – as acceptable. It is possible that each of these psychological tendencies makes us more rather than less reliable. But absent further evidence, it seems more reasonable to distrust beliefs that seem sensitive to self-interest, strong emotion, and rationalization (cf. Sinnott-Armstrong 2006: ch. 9).

Putting these ideas together, the skeptic might argue that in our thinking about ethical questions we behave more like lawyers (seeking to make the best case

---

[12] Prominent arguments that emphasize the epistemic role of problematic psychological influences on our ethical beliefs are offered by Sinnott-Armstrong (2006: ch. 9; 2008; and 2011).

for ourselves) than we do like scientists (seeking the ethical truth).[13] Strikingly, this can be hard to detect from the inside. For example, when we indignantly defend our own interests, our indignation may be self-serving in a way that is often invisible to us.

Next, consider premise 2. Suppose that we grant these influences on our ethical beliefs, and that we at least have reason to worry that such influences make us less reliable. Our next question is: what kind of defeater is this? It is likely that, if these influences are defeaters, they are some combination of undercutting and higher-order defeaters. One reason why it is difficult to be more definitive is that we have not yet said anything specific about what our *evidence* for ethical claims is, and the answer to this question will affect the role of each sort of defeater.

For determinacy, consider the simple idea that that our evidence consists in certain ethical propositions *seeming true* to us. (I consider this view, and competitors to it, in Section 4.) Such seemings would play an epistemic role very similar to perceptual evidence. Recall that in our example of undercutting defeat, the sign undercut our perceptual evidence by suggesting that it might be unreliable in this environment. The psychological pressures at the heart of the first skeptical argument might be claimed to show that our ethical seemings evidence was likewise unreliable, and hence defeated in the same way.

The slogan about behaving more like lawyers than like judges, however, suggests a different basis for a skeptical worry. This is the idea that psychological pressures might tend to make us *misevaluate* the evidence we have. For example we might give too much weight to evidence for hypotheses we would like to accept, and too little weight to evidence against such hypotheses. This is a worry about *higher-order defeat:* the worry is that *even if* we have excellent evidence, we might be unreliable in evaluating it.

Premise 2 claims that these considerations defeat the justification we have for our ethical beliefs. An important question in assessing premise 2 is how strong the relevant influences mentioned are. For example, strong emotion and self-interest can potentially affect our beliefs about any topic. But that surely isn't enough to defeat all of our beliefs. For example, it seems implausible that this could defeat my justification for believing that I am more than three feet tall, or that two is the cube root of eight. If the influences of these factors on some ethical beliefs were similarly modest, that might suggest that they do not defeat our justification for holding ethical beliefs.[14]

---

[13] This adapts a similar slogan offered by Haidt (2001: 821) as a summary of our relevant psychology.

[14] For one example of this sort of response to the debunker, focusing on the influence of disgust on moral judgment, see May (2014).

Another important question in assessing premise 2 concerns the epistemic significance of what I have called "higher-order defeat." I have presented this by suggesting that such evidence can defeat justification, but it is controversial whether higher-order evidence can do this.[15] Consider one way to deny that higher-order evidence can defeat justification. Evidence that I am unreliable about a question is arguably not evidence concerning that question. But one might think that only evidence concerning a question can affect whether I am adequately epistemically justified in believing an answer to that question. So one might think that although higher-order evidence – such as evidence of my unreliability – is unnerving, it cannot defeat my first-order epistemic justification.

How important is this debate about the significance of higher-order evidence for the skeptical argument being considered? This depends on the nature of the evidence for ethical claims. For example, on the seemings view of ethical evidence just mentioned, the skeptic might be able to run their entire argument in terms of undercutting defeat. On a (somewhat surprising) contrasting view, all of our evidence for ethical claims is *non-ethical*, and excellent ethical reasoning is (in part) a matter of drawing ethical conclusions from non-ethical premises alone.[16] A version of the first skeptical argument that targets this sort of view would need to be framed in terms of higher-order defeat.

At this stage, the argument suggests that certain psychological pressures are defeaters for our ethical beliefs. Premise 3 claims that any attempt to confirm our ethical beliefs in the face of these defeaters faces the very same sort of defeater. We can motivate this idea by appealing to two ideas. First, if premise 2 is to be plausible, the defeaters must cast doubt quite generally on the processes that generate ethical beliefs. Second, we cannot confirm our ethical beliefs in ways that avoid those very same processes: after all, how could we confirm an ethical belief except through some sort of ethical reasoning?

In order to resist premise 3, then, one would have to show that there was a way of confirming ethical beliefs that involved very different processes than ordinary ethical reasoning. Several philosophers have made important attempts to offer such methods of confirmation.[17] If successful, some such attempt might show that the first skeptical argument fails to show that ethical knowledge is impossible. However, such a reply allows that this skeptical argument might be

---

[15] For helpful discussion of the options, see Smithies (2019: ch. 9).

[16] See Zimmerman (2010: ch. 5) for discussion of this sort of view.

[17] Consider two examples of methods for the justification of ethical claims that are compatible with our ordinary ethical reasoning being quite unreliable. *Transcendental* arguments (e.g. Korsgaard 1996) and *universalizability* arguments (e.g. Hare 1981) each arrive at ethical conclusions by means that are quite different from our ordinary ethical thinking.

wholly successful in showing that *ordinary* ethical reasoners lack ethical knowledge.

Consider a final important qualification of the first skeptical argument. This qualification can be motivated by returning to our motivating example of undercutting defeat. Suppose that I looked at the red table, but there was no warning sign about the lighting: in this case I would not possess the defeater, and my belief that the table was red would presumably be adequately justified. This is relevant to the import of the first skeptical argument: arguably, most people lack the evidence that is needed to adequately support the first premise of this argument. If so, that argument arguably cannot show that such people's justification for their ethical beliefs is defeated. This argument thus has a somewhat surprising flavor: if successful, it does not *reveal* that you lack adequate justification for your ethical beliefs. Instead, providing you with a strong version of this sort of argument *makes it the case* that you lack such justification.

A second influential class of skeptical arguments arises from worries about the ways that our ethical beliefs can be influenced by forces outside of our own psychologies. We can regiment these worries into our second skeptical argument:

1. Our ethical beliefs are produced in ways that are subject to ideological or evolutionary pressures that are insensitive to ethical truth.
2. The fact mentioned in premise 1 defeats our existing justification for each of our ethical beliefs.
3. The only way to justify our ethical beliefs in the face of this defeater inevitably involves engaging in more ethical reasoning, which is subject to the same defeater.
4. So we lack justification for any of our ethical beliefs.

The overall structure of this argument is very similar to the first. (And again, the defeater in question will be some combination of undercutting and higher-order, depending on the nature of ethical evidence.) So, in what follows, I focus on what is distinctive of this argument. The core worry developed by this argument is that our ethical beliefs arise in certain social and evolutionary circumstances. And we can expect those circumstances to powerfully influence the content of our beliefs in ways indifferent to the truth of those beliefs. Consider two central examples.

First, there are *ideological* pressures on ethical belief. The rich and powerful have disproportionate influence on which ethical ideas are widely circulated. And they have clear interests in promoting ethical ideas that benefit them. When we look at the history of our ethical beliefs, it is not hard to see the role of ethical ideas in preserving ethically objectionable social and political arrangements, such as colonialism, slavery, patriarchy, etc. Similarly, the genesis of much of the European ethical tradition has been entangled with religious belief and controversy. Those suspicious of organized religion might reasonably worry that this entanglement has induced a problematic influence on our ethical beliefs.[18]

Second, there are *evolutionary* pressures on ethical belief. For example, Sharon Street (2006) suggests that it is plausible that evolution has equipped each of us with "basic evaluative tendencies" that, for example, lead each of us to prioritize our own survival and interests, and those of our children and loved ones, over those of strangers. And it is plausible that our ethical beliefs are in turn influenced by these tendencies. These tendencies can be explained precisely because possessing such tendencies would have tended to contribute to our ancestors' reproductive success. In light of this, these tendencies would be selected for, whether or not they accurately represent the ethical facts.

Both ideology and evolution are examples of pressures that plausibly influenced the genesis of our ethical beliefs in ways that are (allegedly) *insensitive* to ethical truth. To see the potential significance of this, it is instructive to contrast an evolutionary explanation of our beliefs about predators, food sources, shelter, etc. in our immediate environment. Here, it looks like it would generally be evolutionarily advantageous for our beliefs to be *sensitive* to the facts that they represent. This is because one's survival will tend to be enhanced by having beliefs which roughly accurately *track* facts about predators, food, etc. For example, consider our beliefs about which foods are poisonous. Where food is scarce, these beliefs tend to promote survival roughly to the extent that they are accurate.

This is not to say that ideology and evolution *necessarily* lead one away from the truth about ethics. For example, if one in fact ought to prioritize the interests of one's children over the interests of strangers, then evolutionary pressures that tend to cause us to believe this will turn out to *help* us to track the truth. But nonetheless, the idea that our beliefs are subject to such influences can appear alarming.

Once again, in evaluating this argument, premises 1 and 2 are the most important. With respect to premise 1, one important question concerns how pervasive these influences are. Here it might seem that the answer is: not that pervasive. For example, evolutionary pressures could not possibly have

---

[18] Classic statements of ideological debunking include Marx and Engels (1970) and Nietzsche (1966). For more recent discussion of ideological debunking, see, for example, Railton (2003: ch. 12).

selected for particular beliefs about how to behave ethically on Twitter. And the same goes for much of our contemporary world, which departs in myriad ways from our primary evolutionary context. Street (2006) has a promising reply to this sort of challenge: as I mentioned above, she suggests that evolution selects for certain *basic evaluative tendencies* which can then structure our thinking about any number of ethical questions.

The central question concerning premise 2 is: why, precisely, should the influence of these pressures on our beliefs serve as an undercutting or higher-order defeater? One idea is that these influences defeat because we have no evidence that they reliably produce true beliefs. But it might seem that we *do* have evidence that these pressures tend to be reliable. To see this, consider the ethical beliefs that seem to you to be most obviously true. Plausibly, lots of those beliefs are influenced by evolution (and/or ideology). And this might seem like evidence that evolution (and/or ideology) *does* in fact generally tend to produce true ethical beliefs. We might try to amend our principle to block this reply: perhaps these influences defeat because we have no evidence that they reliably produce true beliefs, *independent of our ethical beliefs themselves*. But the general form of such a principle appears to lead to general skepticism: for example, we have no evidence of the reliability of our perceptual abilities that does not rely deeply on the use of those very abilities.[19]

A third (and potentially related) route to asymmetrical ethical skepticism appeals to the idea that knowledge of a fact requires that there be an appropriate explanatory connection between the fact and one's belief about it.[20] Some philosophers have found it quite opaque how there could be an explanatory connection between ethical facts and our ethical beliefs. And the sorts of considerations used to motivate the first and second skeptical arguments can also be understood as evidence for lack of an explanatory connection between ethical facts and our beliefs. Suppose, for example, that the best explanation of some ethical belief of mine is that it was produced by self-interested rationalization, or by evolutionary influences. Then it might seem that the ethical facts themselves do not play the right role in explaining that belief.[21]

---

[19] For this point, see Vavova (2018), which also includes much helpful discussion of the epistemic significance of such "irrelevant influences," as she calls them.

[20] For useful discussion of ethical skepticism framed around this sort of idea, see Lutz and Ross (2018).

[21] See Enoch (2011: ch. 7) and Schechter (2018) for the idea that the most promising epistemic challenge based on evolutionary considerations involves an explanatory connection.

We can formulate a third skeptical argument around the idea that there is no appropriate explanatory connection between the ethical facts and our ethical beliefs:

1. There is not an appropriate explanatory connection between our ethical beliefs and the ethical facts.
2. The fact mentioned in premise 1 defeats our existing justification for each of our ethical beliefs.
3. The only way to justify our ethical beliefs in the face of this defeater inevitably involves engaging in more ethical reasoning, which is subject to the same defeater.
4. So we lack justification for any of our ethical beliefs.

The first thing to ask is: why think that lack of explanatory connection is epistemically relevant? This can be motivated by a pair of contrasting examples. I believe there is a pen on my desk. Plausibly, *there being a pen on my desk* directly explains my belief: the pen's being there, coupled with my looking at it, explains why I formed this belief. Other things being equal, this belief amounts to knowledge. By contrast, suppose that it is 10:00 a.m., and I glance at my clock, whose face reads ten o'clock. On this basis, I form the belief that it is 10:00 a.m. However, unbeknownst to me, the clock stopped working at 10:00 p.m. last night (Russell 1948 [2009]). In this case, there does not appear to be the right explanatory connection between the facts about the time and my belief about those facts: I *don't* believe it is 10:00 a.m. *because* it is 10:00 a.m. We can see this because I would have formed the same belief even if I had looked at the clock somewhat earlier or later. In light of this, it is plausible that I lack knowledge of what time it is, despite having a reasonably formed true belief about the time. Further, if you then *show me* that my clock is stopped, this looks like it undercuts my justification for believing that it is 10:00 a.m.

Like the first and second arguments, the third skeptical argument (if successful) is poised to defeat the justification of ethical beliefs among those who come to accept it. However, it is worth noting that the third argument can be developed into a truly general case for skepticism about ethical knowledge. To see this, note that in Russell's stopped-clock case I lacked knowledge even before I noticed that the clock had stopped. This shows that the absence of an explanatory connection can prevent us from having knowledge even if we are unaware of the absence.

The central question for evaluating such an argument is whether our beliefs in fact lack an *appropriate* explanatory connection to ethical facts. One complication here is that it is not easy to precisely state what an appropriate connection is. While the stopped-clock case motivates the idea that the lack of an explanatory connection *can* defeat justification, we sometimes appear to have knowledge without the known fact explaining our beliefs. To see this, consider a simple case: I believe that there is not a competent spy hiding in my ceiling. But if there were such a spy, I would never notice: a *competent* spy wouldn't leave the sorts of clues that I would notice. And so it looks like my belief that there is no such spy is not explained by the absence of such a spy. And yet, it seems very plausible that I am justified in this belief; indeed, it seems plausible that I *know* that there is no such spy. If I am right about this sort of case, then in order to evaluate premise 2 of this argument, we need to get clearer on what constitutes an "appropriate explanatory connection." If premise 2 is to be plausible, there must be some such connection between my belief and the lack of a spy, but no such connection between my belief about the time and my stopped clock. And if premise 1 is to be plausible, it would need to turn out that ethical beliefs fall on the "stopped clock" side of this contrast.

A fourth class of skeptical arguments appeals to the pervasiveness and resilience of *disagreement* in ethics. Focus first on pervasiveness. Ethical disagreement is ubiquitous. For example, you could probably identify ethical disagreements you have with each of your friends and family members, if you probed carefully enough. And if you consider people across cultures and historical periods, the disagreement would appear even more widespread. This appears to be a distinctive fact about ethics: disagreement concerning many other topics is considerably less pervasive.

Next, consider the striking resilience of ethical disagreement. Very often in ethical disagreements, we seem to lack any way to resolve the disagreement that all parties would accept. This contrasts with many non-ethical disagreements. For example, if we divide up the dinner check and get different answers, we can probably agree on a method of checking our work that will settle the matter. If we disagree on the date of Napoleon's abdication, we can probably agree on what sort of authoritative source would settle that. Many ethical disagreements appear immune to such mutually acceptable resolution.

We can appeal to these facts to sketch a fourth skeptical argument:

1. Our ethical beliefs are quite generally subject to pervasive and resilient disagreement.
2. The fact mentioned in premise 1 defeats our existing justification for each of our ethical beliefs.
3. The only way to justify our ethical beliefs inevitably involves engaging in reasoning that appeals to further ethical beliefs, which are subject to the same defeater.
4. So we lack justification for any of our ethical beliefs.

The structure of this argument is again very similar to the previous arguments, so I will focus here on what is different. One central question about premise 2 is: why think that disagreement defeats justification? This idea can be motivated directly by appeal to cases. For example, suppose that you and I set about dividing up the check for our shared dinner. I am pretty good at this sort of thing, so when I finish my calculations I come to believe their results. Then I learn that your calculations came to a slightly different amount. If I know that you are also pretty good at such calculations, news of your results might seem to defeat the justification provided by my own calculations (compare Christensen 2007: 193). After all, I know that one of us made a mistake, and I have no special reason to think that it was you. One might bolster this appeal to cases by appealing to the general plausibility of an epistemic principle denying that beliefs exhibiting certain patterns of disagreement can count as knowledge (e.g. McGrath 2008).

One immediately plausible challenge to premise 2 of this argument concerns the *scope* of the relevant disagreement. The challenge arises from the fact that some ethical claims are not subject to significant controversy. For example, almost everyone believes that, other things being equal, one is not required to kill one's parents. Why should we accept that disagreement about other ethical beliefs defeats the justification of these ethical beliefs? The skeptic might reply to this sort of challenge by appealing to a further story about the relevant defeater. For example, perhaps the reason why the relevant sorts of disagreements defeat is that they are evidence of unreliability (Horn 2017). And perhaps the pervasiveness and resilience of ethical disagreements suggest that our ethical beliefs are unreliable quite generally, in a way that defeats the justification of even seemingly uncontroversial ethical beliefs.[22]

A fifth route to asymmetrical ethical skepticism appeals to the credibility of metaethical views that are hostile to the possibility of ethical knowledge. (Recall that metaethics aims to explain how actual ethical thought and talk – and what [if anything] that thought and talk is distinctively about – fits into reality.)

There are credible arguments for metaethical views which suggest that we are incapable of having ethical knowledge. One influential example of such a view is metaethical error theory. According to the error theorist, our ethical views are systematically false, in much the way that the atheist takes common beliefs about the existence and acts of God to be systematically false.[23]

---

[22] See Locke (2017) for a helpful discussion of the epistemic significance of disagreement in ethics.
[23] Olson (2014) is an excellent orientation to metaethical error theory.

Because evidence for error theory is evidence *against* the truth of each of my ethical beliefs, the credibility of error theory most straightforwardly functions as a *rebutting defeater* for the justification of an ethical belief. This makes the fifth skeptical argument slightly different in structure from the preceding arguments:

1. There are metaethical views, like error theory, which imply that our ethical views are systematically false.
2. Some of these metaethical views are credible enough that we are not justified in believing that they are false.
3. Together, premises 1 and 2 provide a *rebutting defeater* of our justification for each of our ethical beliefs.
4. So we lack adequate justification for any of our ethical beliefs.

Premise 1 is relatively uncontroversial. And premise 3 is close to trivial. This is because premise 2 in effect says that the relevant views are credible enough to show that there is a rebutting defeater. Premise 3 makes explicit the implications of there existing such views. Notice that a hypothesis doesn't need to be *known* in order to show that there is a rebutting defeater. To see this, suppose that I believe that I left my keys on the counter, but then you say you think they are in the bathroom. I do not need to *know* that you are correct for your testimony to defeat my justification. Rather, your testimony only needs to be credible enough that I cannot rule out this competing hypothesis about the location of my keys.

If this is right, the central question for this argument is whether we should accept premise 2. This rests in large part on how credible the arguments for views like error theory are. Notice that arguments for views like error theory do not need to show that error theory is true in order to support ethical skepticism. They merely need to be credible enough that we are not adequately justified in believing competing ethical claims.[24]

A final important class of arguments for ethical skepticism takes certain metaphysical theses as central premises. To see how such arguments work, I will focus on a specific example. Many philosophers think that if I *ought* to perform an action, I must be *able* to perform it. For example, suppose that, after an accident, I could save someone's life if I could lift a large truck off of their leg. Plausibly, it would not be true that I ought to lift the truck, because I could not: it is simply too heavy for me to lift. Or suppose that someone pushes me off a building, and I am unable to avoid falling on you: given that I could not avoid falling on you, it seems that I did not do something wrong by falling on you. It is

---

[24] It is relatively rare for philosophers to discuss the epistemic significance of credible but not decisive arguments for error theory. An important exception is Sinnott-Armstrong (2006: ch. 3).

possible to mount metaphysical arguments that I am never able to perform any action that I do not perform. For example, consider the view that everything that I do is *determined* by the combination of the conditions of the world at some previous time (which I had no control over) and the laws of nature. It might seem that if this is true, I am never able to do anything other than what I in fact do. Call this view *nihilism about ability*. As with arguments for metaethical error theory, such metaphysical arguments have struck many philosophers as credible.

This puts me in a position to sketch a sixth skeptical argument, structurally similar to the fifth:

1. There are metaphysical views, like nihilism about ability, which imply that large classes of our ethical beliefs are false.
2. Some of these metaphysical views are credible enough that we are not justified in believing that they are false.
3. Together, 1 and 2 provide a *rebutting defeater* to our justification for each of our ethical beliefs in the relevant classes.
4. So we lack adequate justification for ethical beliefs in the relevant classes.

It is worth noting that the skepticism suggested by this argument is more limited in scope than that defended by the previous arguments: for instance, this sort of argument does not in any obvious way impugn our judgments about which outcomes are ethically better or worse than others.

It is also worth emphasizing that this is merely an example of a general skeptical strategy: other metaphysical premises could potentially be used to defend different skeptical conclusions about ethics.[25] Evidently, the central question for skeptics pursuing this sort of strategy is whether there are credible metaphysical views that have these sorts of implications for our ethical views. Notice that one might challenge the credibility of the relevant view (for example, by arguing that we do have non-trivial abilities), or by denying that such metaphysical views have the ethical implications claimed (for example, by denying that ability is a condition on ethical obligation).

I have just presented six skeptical strategies separately. I did this for the sake of clarity. However, it may be that the most compelling case for asymmetrical ethical skepticism involves combining some or all of these elements into a more complex argument (Jones 2006: 66; Sinnott-Armstrong 2006). There are at least three ways that combining skeptical arguments might strengthen them. First, they might each provide independent support for a skeptical conclusion.

---

[25] It is comparatively rare to argue in the relatively simple way suggested in the argument above. Relevant arguments tend to arise within the large literature discussing nihilism about moral responsibility (see e.g. Caruso [2018], especially section 3.3 for the connection to morality).

Second, considerations from one argument might strengthen another argument. For example, one might argue that the fact of pervasive ethical disagreement is further evidence for a lack of an explanatory connection between ethical facts and ethical beliefs (see Mackie 1977, 36–38 for a related argument). Third, some skeptical arguments might be more powerful when applied to some ethical beliefs than to others. For example, I have just mentioned that beliefs about value may escape the argument from metaphysics I have just sketched. And certain ethical beliefs may be *cultural universals*, against which arguments from disagreement may be weaker. If different skeptical arguments can be shown to be independently credible, the skeptical upshot of their combination may be harder to reasonably resist than any one of the arguments by itself.

I conclude this section by considering the implications of ethical skepticism for the methodology of ethics. One might think that the implication is clear: ethical inquiry is impossible. However, this would be too quick. First, note that the conclusion that we cannot achieve *adequate* epistemic justification is compatible with certain ethical claims being epistemically justified *to some extent*. It is thus compatible with a methodology that seeks to put us in a position to achieve *better* justified ethical beliefs. Further, as many philosophers have noted, ethical inquiry is distinctively *practically relevant*: we often ask ethical questions in order to decide how to live. And such an inquiry could (and on some views inevitably will) survive ethical skepticism. Consider one example: the argument from the credibility of metaethical error theory. Even if this argument deprives us of adequate epistemic justification for our ethical beliefs, it does not serve to change the *relative* credibility of various ethical claims. And it thus may be irrelevant for the methodologist engaged in ethical inquiry in order to guide her decisions (cf. Ross 2006).

I have focused here on arguments that conclude that we lack the sort of justification needed for ethical knowledge. However, as I noted in Section 2.1, it is possible to argue for more or less ambitious skeptical conclusions. For example, a more ambitious skeptic might seek to offer arguments that claim to show that we have no more justification to believe any ethical thesis than any consistent alternative. This conclusion may put pressure on the methodologist to find a *non-epistemic* basis by which to evaluate alternative ethical claims. We will return to this idea in Section 5.

2.3 Anti-Skeptical Resources

Thus far, I have focused on introducing the most important and influential bases for asymmetrical skepticism about ethics. The initial plausibility of these bases helps to explain why asymmetrical ethical skepticism can seem more credible than skepticism with a completely general scope. But skeptical arguments in ethics can and have been vigorously resisted. This section introduces a collection of important resources and strategies for resisting them. I begin by introducing four influential views in general epistemology which can complicate the ethical skeptic's arguments. I discuss the use of three influential general anti-skeptical strategies against the ethical skeptic. I then introduce an important foil for the skeptic's view, which I call "epistemically modest non-skepticism." I conclude the section by considering the use of metaethical theory as an anti-skeptical resource.

Asymmetrical ethical skepticism is a thesis about the availability of epistemic justification adequate for knowledge. Because of this, certain general views about knowledge and epistemic justification can have important implications for the prospects of skeptical arguments in ethics. I offer four brief examples.

First, consider an influential theory of the semantics of epistemic terms: epistemic contextualism.[26] According to the contextualist, words like 'know' are context-sensitive, where this means that they make a different contribution to the truth conditions of sentences in different contexts of use. To see this idea, consider a paradigm context-sensitive expression: the word 'tall.' Consider the sentence 'This baby giraffe is tall' uttered during a visit to the zoo. If this sentence is uttered in a context where we are comparing baby animals at the zoo, it is true. In a context where we are comparing giraffes, however, the very same sentence is false. On one standard way of modeling epistemic contextualism, a conversational context will include a set of relevant alternatives for a given proposition P. A sentence of the form 'S knows that P' is true in a context just in case the believer S is in a position to rule out the alternatives to P that are relevant in that context of assessment. If true, epistemic contextualism has important implications for how we assess ethical skepticism. To see why, consider an arbitrary ethical proposition E. In ordinary contexts, it may be that in order for a sentence of the form 'S knows that E' to be true, S needs only be able to rule out certain other ordinary ethical claims that are incompatible with E, which we may often be in a position to do. On the other hand, when a skeptic makes a skeptical argument, this may often have the effect of expanding the set of relevant alternatives in the context, thereby making it the case that sentences of the form 'S knows that E' are quite generally false in that context.

---

[26] For an introduction to epistemic contextualism, see Rysiew (2016).

Second, consider epistemic coherentism.[27] This is a thesis about the structure of epistemic justification. A standard type of coherentist claims that the justification of any given belief a person has is a function of its relationship to the maximally coherent subset of that person's beliefs. What makes my belief that I have hands highly justified, on this account, is the many connections this belief bears to my other beliefs. By contrast, what makes my belief that the sun is made of plasma poorly justified is that it is barely connected at all to my other beliefs. Coherentism is generally understood to be hostile to global skepticism. After all, given coherentism, for global skepticism to be true of a believer, that believer would need to wholly lack a highly coherent subset of beliefs.[28] Coherentism is clearly compatible with asymmetrical ethical skepticism: most saliently, our ethical beliefs could fail to cohere appropriately with each other, or with the rest of our beliefs. Indeed, many of the arguments considered in Section 2.2 could be understood as challenging the coherence of our ethical beliefs with our other beliefs. But even here, coherentism might seem to make justification easier to come by. This is because it is at least initially plausible that many of us have ethical beliefs that are part of a reasonably coherent overall body of beliefs.

Third, consider a competing view about the structure of epistemic justification: foundationalism.[29] The foundationalist claims that some beliefs are epistemically justified by something other than their relationship to other beliefs: they are justificationally basic. Consider an example that motivates foundationalism. Suppose that I glance out my window and see a bird flying. It seems plausible that I am now justified in believing that there is a bird flying outside my window. And it seems plausible that this newly justified belief is justified by something other than my prior beliefs. Perhaps, for example, it is justified by the character of my experience when I looked out the window, or perhaps it is justified by my being in an appropriate relationship to the flying bird. One important question for the epistemic foundationalist is how to characterize the justifiers for basic beliefs. And here there looms a potential route to asymmetrical ethical skepticism not faced by the coherentist: to deny that any ethical beliefs are basic, or justified by their relation to beliefs that are basic. (Recall the regress argument for general skepticism, briefly mentioned in Section 2.2. The argument now being considered is in effect a local regress argument for asymmetrical ethical skepticism.) This has led some non-skeptical

---

[27] For an introduction to epistemic coherentism, see Olsson (2017).

[28] However, for an important model for combining coherentism and skepticism, see Sinnott-Armstrong (2006).

[29] For an introduction to epistemic foundationalism, see Hasan and Fumerton (2018).

epistemologists of ethics to argue systematically for a theory of basic beliefs that is expansive enough to include basic ethical beliefs.[30]

Finally, consider stakes-sensitive accounts of adequate epistemic justification. On such accounts, the practical stakes facing an agent who would like to rely on a certain belief can affect how much evidence is required to adequately justify that belief. For example: suppose that I noticed several weeks ago that my bank was open on Saturdays. On stakes-sensitive accounts, whether I now know on this basis that the bank is open this coming Saturday in part rests on the choices I face. If acting on the belief that the bank is open when it is in fact closed would be a disaster for me, then I need a lot of evidence that the bank is open to make it rational to rely on the bank's being open in my practical deliberation. On a standard form of the stakes-sensitive view, if I would act irrationally by relying on the bank being open, then I do not know that it is open. Stakes-sensitivity by itself seems unlikely to support or undermine ethical skepticism, since ethical beliefs vary substantially in the practical stakes of relying on them. However, the stakes-sensitive account might suggest the disturbing possibility that we tend to lack ethical knowledge in exactly those situations in which the most hangs on which ethical beliefs we rely on in choosing to act.[31]

The general theories just briefly sketched are important to the evaluation of skeptical arguments in ethics. However, as I have emphasized, they are not primarily tools to use to rebut the skeptic. I now shift focus to consider three specifically anti-skeptical strategies.

The most straightforward way of resisting any given skeptical argument is to directly critique that argument. For example, consider the schematic arguments presented in Section 2.2. It is not at all trivial to develop any one of them into a persuasive case that we lack adequately justified ethical belief. Because there are many ways that an argument can fail, it is impossible to catalogue all such possible critiques. However, there are two important general anti-skeptical strategies that it is useful to keep in mind when considering whether we can have ethical knowledge.

One classic anti-skeptical strategy is to argue that the skeptic's argument is *self-undermining*. For example, consider the following simplistic skeptical argument:

1. No one should accept any claim about which intelligent people disagree.
2. Intelligent people disagree about very many ethical claims.
3. One should not accept any of these ethical claims.

---

[30] See, for example, Huemer (2005: ch. 5) and Enoch (2011: ch. 3).

[31] For an introduction to stakes–sensitivity in epistemology, see Kim (2017).

This is a kind of disagreement-based argument. One problem with this argument is that many intelligent people disagree with premise 1 of this argument. In light of this, premise 1 seems to instruct us not to accept itself! Given this, it is hard to see why we should accept the conclusion of the simplistic skeptical argument. (For a case that many disagreement-based arguments for moral skepticism are self-undermining, see Sampson (2019)).

A second classic anti-skeptical strategy was suggested by G. E. Moore. On one way of reading Moore, he observes that certain of our beliefs are more credible than the conclusion of any possible argument against them. Given this greater credibility, the Moorean characteristically claims that it is more reasonable to reject any such argument than it is to abandon the highly credible belief (cf. Moore 1903; 1959 ch. 9). Notice that in offering such a reply to a skeptical argument, the Moorean does not (necessarily) offer any *explanation* of what has gone wrong with that argument.

The Moorean reply might seem like an invitation to unreasonable dogmatism: now we don't need to engage with arguments just because we happen to find the conclusion of those arguments incredible? But sometimes the Moorean reaction appears extremely reasonable. Consider an example. There you are, staring at the five fingers of your left hand, while Sophistical Sal gives you an amazing argument for the conclusion that you have only three fingers on that hand. The argument is ingenious; you cannot identify a flaw in it. But you are staring at your fingers, and it would surely be unreasonable to suspend judgment that they are there. It is manifestly obvious that *something* went wrong with Sal's argument, even if you have no idea what.

One might try to identify extremely credible ethical claims to levy against the ethical skeptic in a Moorean argument. For example:

(17) It is (*at least* a little bit) bad to violently assault random strangers on a daily basis.

(18) Brushing my teeth this morning was not the worst thing anyone has ever done.

The Moorean might propose that these claims are as credible or certain as the claim that I have five fingers on my left hand. Appealing to such claims, the Moorean anti-skeptic about ethics can conclude that we can rest confident that something is wrong with any argument for skepticism about all ethical claims, even if we have no idea what (for discussion, see McPherson 2009).

Focus next on the fact that we are considering arguments for *asymmetrical* ethical skepticism. Given this ambition, an important kind of reply to such arguments will be to show that they *overgeneralize*. It is useful to distinguish two different ways that a skeptical argument might overgeneralize:

- it might imply an implausible skepticism about some non-ethical topic
- it might generalize to an argument for global skepticism.

You might wonder: why is it an objection to an argument for ethical skepticism that it generalizes in one of these ways? If the argument is sound, this just shows that it is more powerful than its author realized! One answer to this question is suggested by the Moorean approach just introduced. It is controversial whether ethical claims like (17)–(18) are immune to skeptical doubt. So someone who accepts Moore's arguments against the global skeptic might reject a Moorean argument against ethical skepticism. But if any Moorean arguments work, then global skepticism is false. And if we know that global skepticism is false, then we are in a position to know that any argument that entails global skepticism is unsound. There is also a more modest form of the overgeneralization objection. I opened this section with reasons to think that the epistemology of ethics was in some way distinctively puzzling or problematic. Arguments for asymmetrical ethical skepticism might hope to capitalize on that appearance. If those arguments generalize to throw all of our beliefs into question, they are no longer apt explanations of the *distinctively* puzzling epistemic character of ethics.

Consider an example of how an overgeneralization objection might proceed. The third skeptical argument discussed in Section 2.2 appeals to the idea that knowledge requires an explanatory connection to the known facts. Many philosophers have taken it to be plausible that *mathematical* facts do not explain beliefs. (Consider: how, precisely, could the fact that 2+2=4 explain my belief in that fact?) This means that mathematics is potentially a *companion in guilt* for ethics, when considering this skeptical argument. A companion in guilt response to an objection proceeds in two steps. First, it argues that if the objection succeeds against its intended target, it would also succeed against some other target: the "companion." Second, it argues that the objection is not plausible against the companion. Mathematics is a powerful companion in guilt in reply to skeptical arguments in ethics, precisely because it is extremely credible that we have knowledge of mathematical facts like 2+2=4.[32]

One striking feature of asymmetrical ethical skepticism is that it is an *extreme view*: it doesn't say that we have *little* adequately justified ethical belief; it says that we have *none*. We can think of this sort of ethical skepticism as one end of a continuum of views about the possibility of adequately justified ethical belief. At the one end is ethical skepticism. At the other end is the hypothesis that adequately justified ethical belief is extremely easy to come by across a wide

---

[32] See Lillehammer (2007) for a detailed discussion of companions in guilt arguments.

range of cases. It is important to notice that there are a range of views between these extremes. I want to focus on one such view, which I take to be a powerful foil for the skeptic. This is the view that adequately justified ethical belief is possible, but we are in general poorly equipped to get it. Call this view *epistemically modest non-skepticism* about ethics.[33]

Modest non-skepticism can be motivated by reflecting on our ordinary epistemic practices in ethics. On the one hand, I initially motivated ethical skepticism by appealing to apparent epistemic asymmetries between ethics and other topics. This asymmetry also appears well explained by modest non-skepticism. And alongside the oddity of reporting ethical discoveries, we can note the *normalcy* of making ethical assertions and accepting ethical testimony from trusted speakers. This combination suggests that our implicit assumptions about ethics may be that we have some ethical knowledge, but it is very hard to make ethical discoveries that extend that knowledge to controversial cases in a credible way. This suggests that perhaps modest non-skepticism should be our default position in the epistemology of ethics.

I have framed epistemically modest non-skepticism as a foil for the skeptic, but it is also a foil for more optimistic views about our epistemic prospects in ethics. And here it has some advantages over the skeptic. For example, the anti-skeptical strategies are at least less clearly applicable against it. The clearest case is the Moorean strategy. The modest non-skeptic can simply *grant* that we have the little bits of ethical knowledge that the Moorean points to. Indeed, modest non-skepticism is arguably a natural view for the Moorean to accept. For an influential gloss on the Moorean perspective suggests humility about what philosophical argument or inquiry can achieve (e.g. Fine 2001, 2). If we suppose that our primary means of ethical inquiry involves distinctively philosophical methods, then Moorean humility about philosophy might suggest pessimism about what we can achieve in ethical inquiry.[34] Because of this, modest non-skepticism is an important foil for more optimistic views about the epistemology of ethics.

The modest non-skeptic might also claim that her view is supported by the sorts of evidence used by the skeptical arguments discussed in Section 2.2. For example, certain challenges to our ethical beliefs might most plausibly apply only selectively to those beliefs. Let me illustrate this idea with two examples.

First, Derek Parfit famously argued that the correct theory of personal identity, and related theses in metaphysics, made certain views in ethics more

---

[33] Wedgwood (2014) gives a very similar name to a similar but slightly more optimistic view.
[34] For relevant discussion, see McPherson (2015a; 2018b).

credible than they otherwise appear, and other views less credible (1984). Compared to the metaphysical argument for skepticism considered above, Parfit's conclusion is both more epistemically modest and more selective among ethical theories.

Second, several philosophers have argued that only an identifiable subset of our ethical beliefs is systematically vulnerable to defeat on the basis of the sorts of considerations mentioned in the first two skeptical arguments. For example, Joshua Greene (2007) argues that unreliable psychological processes defeat the justification of our *deontological* ethical beliefs (notably, those which place ethical constraints on our bringing about good effects) without defeating the justification of our *consequentialist* beliefs. If successful, this would suggest that consequentialist ethical views are better justified than many believe, by undermining the credibility of an important competing view.[35]

These examples illustrate the point that debunking arguments in ethics need not entail ethical skepticism. In these examples, the authors take the defeaters they identify to remove misleading evidence, allowing us to identify the correct systematic ethical theory (for critical discussion, see e.g. Kahane 2011).

A final potential strategy for replying to arguments for asymmetrical ethical skepticism involves appeal to metaethical theorizing. The core idea here is straightforward. As we have seen, some metaethical theories, such as error theory, are unfriendly to ethical knowledge. However, other metaethical theories are distinctively friendly to the possibility of ethical knowledge. That is, if we can come to know that one of these theories is true, that would provide a basis for rejecting both skepticism and epistemic modesty about ethics.

Consider an illustrative example. One view about ethical thought is *simple subjectivism*. According to this view, what it is for someone to judge that x is good is for that person to believe that she approves of x. Such a belief will be true just in case the believer in fact approves of x. Because of this, simple subjectivism makes ethical knowledge *extremely* easy to come by. Indeed, knowing that simple subjectivism is true would function to rebut almost any of the arguments for ethical skepticism we have considered thus far. Of course, simple subjectivism is not a plausible metaethic. However, many metaethicists have defended metaethical theories which are like simple subjectivism in making ethical knowledge relatively easy to come by.[36]

---

[35] See also Singer (2005) and Huemer (2008) for examples of non-skeptical debunking in ethics.

[36] See Stojanovic (2018) for an introduction to relativist metaethical views.

The skeptic might reply to this sort of resource by denying that we are in a position to know which *metaethical* theory is true. That might be so. But notice that if the skeptic replies in this way, then they have in effect broadened the scope of their skeptical argument: they now need to defend at least a limited metaethical skepticism alongside their ethical skepticism. This is important because not all of the arguments for *ethical* skepticism can be smoothly adapted into arguments for metaethical skepticism. This broadening thus potentially complicates the ethical skeptic's task.

This section has aimed to make vivid the range of potential bases for skepticism about ethics, as well as the variety of anti-skeptical strategies available. In both cases, my aim has been to provide a clear and illustrative introduction, not an exhaustive survey: the topic is too large and too complex for that.

The examples of subjectivism and error theory discussed in this section begin to illustrate the deep connections between the epistemology of ethics and metaethics. In this section I have considered epistemic implications of this connection. In Section 3, I shift focus, and show how – if we assume that we can have ethical knowledge – these connections can be used to inform our evaluation of candidate metaethical theories.

3 Epistemic Considerations in Metaethics

Return to the example of metaethical error theory. According to the error theorist, our ethical views are systematically false. As I explained in Section 2, the credibility of error theory forms the basis for an elegant argument for ethical skepticism. But it is possible to turn this argument on its head. Suppose that one *knew* that one had ethical knowledge. Perhaps, for example, one knew this by reflecting on the certainty of examples like:

(17) It is (*at least* a little bit) bad to violently assault random strangers on a daily basis.

Then one would have a simple and powerful argument against error theory:

1. If error theory is true, then we have no ethical knowledge.
2. We have ethical knowledge (of theses like (17)).
3. Error theory is not true.

Given the range and potency of arguments for ethical skepticism (such as those introduced in Section 2), one might be suspicious of premise 2. But if good grounds can be offered for this premise, it appears that we can use this argument to rule out an important metaethical view.[37]

---

[37] See McPherson (2009) for discussion of this sort of argument.

More generally, if ethical skepticism can be defeated, then we likely have both ethical knowledge and some grasp on the nature of that knowledge. The argument against error theory illustrates how such knowledge could be metaethically significant. This section explains how both the existence and nature of ethical knowledge can be used to argue against many of the most prominent metaethical theories. Many of the arguments considered in this section are closely related to arguments discussed in Section 2. As we shall see, the very considerations that some have treated as the bases of skeptical arguments can instead be used in arguments for metaethical conclusions.

I begin by considering an extremely influential argument due to Sharon Street.[38] As we saw in Section 2, Street argues that evolutionary pressures have selected for "basic evaluative tendencies" because possession of those tendencies tends to contribute to reproductive success, and *not* because they accurately represent the (alleged) ethical facts. In Section 2, we saw how this idea could contribute to an argument for ethical skepticism. However, that skeptical argument depends crucially on certain metaethical assumptions.

To see this, consider one of the views discussed at the close of Section 2: simple subjectivism. According to simple subjectivism, someone's belief that x is good is true just in case that person approves of x. Given simple subjectivism, the thesis that my ethical beliefs were shaped by evolutionary pressures in the way that Street suggests is no defeater to my ethical knowledge. This is because this evolutionary thesis does nothing to suggest that my ethical beliefs are not reliably linked to my attitudes of approval. And according to simple subjectivism, such a link makes my ethical beliefs reliable guides to the truth.

As we saw in Section 2, there are important arguments for the conclusion that we possess ethical knowledge. Such arguments, however, do not make evolutionary pressures disappear. Indeed, the thesis that we have ethical knowledge can be combined with claims about such pressures to provide an interesting argument for a metaethical conclusion. This argument takes as its foil the idea that there are ethical facts that are independent of our evaluative attitudes. Many metaethicists have accepted this view. They think that ethical facts are more like biological facts (which are what they are whatever we think of them) than they are like facts about what is tasty (which plausibly depend in some way on our tastes). I will follow Street in calling this sort of view "realism." (I use scare

---

[38] Joyce (2006) offers an important similar argument that has to some extent been neglected in the vast ensuing literature.

quotes here to mark that it is controversial precisely what makes a metaethical view count as realist).[39]

I set aside several complexities in Street's actual argument in providing the following Street-inspired argument against "realism":

1. Our ethical beliefs are subject to striking pressures that would make them insensitive to ethical truth, if ethical "realism" were true.
2. The fact mentioned in premise 1 would defeat our justification for each of our ethical beliefs, if ethical "realism" were true.
3. So, if ethical "realism" were true, we would not be adequately justified in believing any ethical claims.
4. But we are adequately justified in believing some ethical claims.
5. So ethical "realism" is not true.

As with the second skeptical argument considered in Section 2, the specifically *evolutionary* basis we have been considering is not essential to the style of anti-realist argument just offered. For example, the striking pressures mentioned in premise 1 of this argument could be due to ideology or random developments in intellectual fashion rather than evolution.

Many of the same complications and controversies facing the second skeptical argument apply to this argument as well. However, there is at least one additional dimension of complexity here: precisely *which* metaethical views (if any) are vulnerable to this sort of argument. While Street argues that the argument is potent against all realist views, some have argued that at least some naturalistic realist views have distinctive resources for escaping the argument (e.g. Copp 2008; see Street 2008 for a reply).

In the literature that flowered following the publication of Street's paper, enormous attention has focused on related epistemic arguments that target a more specific view than realism: "non-naturalism" about the metaphysics of ethics. Precisely how to understand what ethical non-naturalism amounts to is controversial.[40] However, the epistemic challenge we will consider most clearly targets views with two features. First, on the target views, ethical properties are independent of our attitudes. Second, on the target views ethical properties are causally inert. To mark both the standard association of these ideas with non-naturalism and the controversy, I will refer to the target views using scare quotes, like this: *"non-naturalism."*

The relevant epistemic challenge for the "non-naturalist" is this: If ethical facts are independent of our ethical beliefs and attitudes, then facts about our

---

[39] See Dunaway (2018) for an introduction to realism and objectivity in the metaethical context.

[40] For contrasting informative proposals for distinguishing naturalism from non-naturalism, see McPherson (2015d) and Rosen (2018).

ethical beliefs and attitudes do not explain the ethical facts (as they would, for example, if simple subjectivism were true). And if ethical facts are causally inert, then it seems that they could not explain why we have the ethical beliefs and attitudes that we do. This is because it seems like these beliefs and attitudes would be fully explained by whatever caused them to come into existence. In short, "non-naturalism" can seem to ensure that there is no explanatory connection between our ethical beliefs and the ethical facts.

This means that we can construct an argument against "non-naturalism" that adapts the third skeptical argument considered in Section 2. This argument claimed that the lack of an explanatory connection was a barrier to knowledge. Appropriately adapted, the argument can be formulated this way:

1. If "non-naturalism" is true, there is not an appropriate explanatory connection between our ethical beliefs and the ethical facts.
2. If "non-naturalism" is true, premise 1 defeats our justification for each of our ethical beliefs.
3. But we have some adequately justified ethical beliefs.
4. So "non-naturalism" is not true.

As the vast ensuing literature has shown, how best to develop and evaluate arguments of this broad kind is an extremely vexed matter.[41]

The appearance that we can have ethical knowledge or evidence can also present challenges for "anti-realist" metaethical views. One prominent form of anti-realism in ethics is *non-cognitivism*. On this sort of view, what it is to accept an ethical claim is to be in a *non-cognitive* state; a state that is more like a desire than it is like a belief.[42]

A straightforward epistemic worry about this view is that epistemic categories like knowledge or evidence do not seem to apply to non-cognitive states. For example, contrast the following questions:

Q1. What evidence does Ali have for his belief that there are cookies here?
Q2. What evidence does Miryam have for her desire that there are cookies here?

Q1 is felicitous, but Q2 seems puzzling or confused. And the same is true quite generally for questions about evidence supporting non-cognitive states. But ethical claims *do* appear to be apt targets for epistemic evaluation. So this appears to count against non-cognitivism. Non-cognitivists have typically addressed this sort of worry by arguing that while acceptance of an ethical

---

[41] For a helpful introduction to these arguments, see Schechter (2018).

[42] For a brief introduction to non-cognitivism, see Bedke (2018); for a book-length introduction, see Schroeder (2010).

claim is like desiring in some respects, it is also like believing in certain important respects, in ways that allegedly allow the non-cognitivist to explain the applicability of epistemic categories to ethics.

A more sophisticated epistemic objection to non-cognitivism is that it seems to license a kind of *wishful thinking*. Consider the following argument (Dorr 2002):

1. If lying is wrong, the souls of liars will be punished in the afterlife.
2. Lying is wrong.
3. The souls of liars will be punished in the afterlife.

Intuitively, it seems plausible that someone could justifiably accept premise 1, come to justifiably accept premise 2, and on that basis come to be justified in accepting the conclusion of this argument. This looks like it would be an instance of good reasoning. But suppose that non-cognitivism is true. Then coming to accept premise 2 would be the acquiring of a new non-cognitive attitude. In such a case, inferring premise 3 on the basis of this argument appears to involve inferring a factual conclusion on the basis of acquiring a non-cognitive attitude. But that *doesn't* look like good reasoning. Rather, it looks like it an illegitimate inference, akin to wishful thinking. In a slogan, if non-cognitivism were true, then certain (in fact legitimate) inferences would be illegitimate. So non-cognitivism is false.

Notice a contrast between this wishful thinking argument and the arguments discussed previously in this section. The preceding arguments appealed to very modest epistemic premises: that we can have ethical knowledge or evidence. By contrast, the wishful thinking argument appeals to specific epistemic texture: the idea that justification can be transmitted to non-ethical conclusions by good reasoning in part from ethical premises.

We can generalize from this example: it is plausibly not enough for a metaethic to vindicate the possibility of ethical knowledge. Rather, a metaethic must be compatible with what we know about the epistemology of ethics, besides the (alleged) existence of ethical knowledge. In short, metaethics must be compatible with the *distinctive epistemic character* of ethics. Consider two further examples of how this might matter for evaluating metaethical theories.

First, return to simple subjectivism. As I emphasized in Section 2, simple subjectivism makes ethical knowledge easy to acquire. The way in which it does so, however, renders simple subjectivism strikingly implausible. To see this, suppose that you are trying to determine whether it is wrong to eat meat. According to simple subjectivism, you can settle this question by simply asking yourself how you feel about eating meat (provided that you know you can reliably figure out how you feel by introspection). This seems to make answering this ethical question *too* easy. Further, imagine that, faced with this question, you search for considerations that favor one answer or the other, marshal them into arguments, and seek to carefully and fairly evaluate those arguments. On simple subjectivism, this is an epistemically misguided activity, in roughly the way that similar reasoning would be misguided in seeking to determine whether you find chocolate tasty. These epistemic implications count heavily against the plausibility of simple subjectivism as a metaethic.

Second, consider naturalistic ethical realism. Roughly, on this view, ethical facts are independent of our attitudes, and are of a kind, metaphysically speaking, with the sorts of facts investigated by the natural and social sciences.[43] This view can seem hard to square with the fact that the investigation of fundamental ethical questions appears to be more a matter of armchair reasoning than of carefully constructed empirical study. This leaves the naturalist with an epistemic puzzle: if ethical facts are of a kind with paradigmatic naturalistic facts, why does it appear that the best means of investigating these types of facts are so very different?[44]

Adequately capturing the distinctive epistemic character of ethics is thus an important constraint on the plausibility of metaethical theories. However, this raises an important question: *what is* the distinctive epistemic character of ethics? The next section takes up this question.

4 The Epistemic Character of Ethics

Return to the example with which I opened this Element: my coming to the conclusion that I shouldn't eat meat. Considered in very general terms, the process by which I came to this conclusion is not at all distinctive: I had some experiences (notably of catching, killing, and then eating fish), reflected on those experiences, did some reasoning, and drew a conclusion. Thoughtful people come to conclusions about a very wide variety of topics this way, all of the time. But it is easy to suspect that this apparent similarity is superficial: that if we examine the case more carefully, we will find that our ways of coming to ethical knowledge are really quite different from our ways of acquiring knowledge of other kinds.

So far, our discussion has focused overwhelmingly on the *possibility* of ethical knowledge. The skeptical arguments in Section 2 challenged the possibility of such knowledge, while the arguments in Section 3 explored

---

[43] Again, for more developed – but still controversial – characterizations of naturalistic realism, see McPherson (2015d) and Rosen (2018).

[44] For discussion of this question, see McPherson (2018b).

possible metaethical implications of such knowledge. The possibility of ethical knowledge is a matter of considerable interest. But if we assume that ethical knowledge is possible, this raises two pressing questions. If ethical knowledge is possible, how is it possible? And if ethics has a distinctive epistemic character, what is that character?

This section takes up these two questions. I focus much of the section on the two main classes of answer to the "how possible" question, which appeal to empirical (Section 4.2) and a priori (Section 4.3) sources of ethical justification, respectively. I then consider an apparently striking way that the epistemology of ethics is distinctive: the idea that there is something problematic about relying on ethical testimony (Section 4.4). I conclude by considering the general structure of the relationship between the epistemology of ethics and general epistemology (Section 4.5). I begin by clarifying the "how possible" question.

4.1 Clarifying the Target Epistemic Questions

Suppose for the moment that you think that we can get ethical knowledge by testimony (we will come back to this question in Section 4.4). For example, suppose that you are not sure how you ought to handle your boss's abrasive and sometimes offensive manner. Suppose that you ask a wise and trusted friend, and believe their claims about what you should do. This seems like it might be a straightforward and familiar way of getting ethical knowledge. However, it cannot explain how ethical knowledge is possible. This is because, in general, testimonial evidence is only good if the testifier knows what they are talking about. I'm a good source of testimonial evidence concerning my birthdate, but not your mom's birthdate, precisely because I know my birthdate, and I may have no idea about when your mom was born. But now consider your trusted friend. How did *they* come to know how you ought to respond to your boss? If we appeal again to testimony, we just push the question back to our friend's source. This shows that ethical knowledge seemingly could not be testimonial "all the way down." And if not, testimony does not suffice to explain how ethical knowledge could be possible.

It might also seem like we can acquire ethical knowledge by simply investigating prosaic facts. For example, if you came to understand your boss's personality, you might be able to predict how they will react to being confronted about their offensive talk. And that, in turn, might be crucial to figuring out how you ought to react to your boss. It will make all the ethical difference whether they are the sort of person who respects fair-minded personal criticism, or an emotionally fragile and vindictive tyrant.

The best reply to this idea appeals to a thesis about the structure of ethical justification: our knowledge of many ethical claims plausibly rests on our knowledge of certain other claims, some of which are ethical and some of which are not. Suppose that you come to know that you should *not* politely criticize your boss. This will likely be because you come to know facts like the following:

(non-ethical) Your boss will react to any criticism by making all of your co-workers miserable for the foreseeable future.
(ethical) Other things being equal, you shouldn't do something that will lead to a lot of avoidable misery for many people.

No amount of knowledge of your boss's personality can justify belief in (ethical). And you need to know (ethical) to know how you ought to react to your boss. So prosaic investigation of your boss's personality is seemingly not the sort of thing that can explain how ethical knowledge is possible.

Another lesson of this example is that some ethical claims are apparently more *epistemically basic* than others, in the following sense: we can typically come to know the latter by coming to know the former, and not vice versa. For example, (ethical) appears more basic than the claim that you shouldn't politely criticize your boss in this case.

One important question about the character of the epistemology of ethics is *how general* the most epistemically basic ethical claims are. Here we can distinguish several possibilities. Some ethical propositions are *highly* general, such as:

(18) Actions are right just in case and because they are the option, among those available to the agent, that maximizes human happiness.

Some propositions are less general but still have very broad scope. For example:

(19) There is always a strong ethical reason against breaking a promise.

Much ethical discussion concerns "cases," which are typically lightly sketched scenarios or "thought experiments" intended to elicit a clear ethical judgment. A classic example is Judith Thomson's *transplant* case (1985). To simplify the case:

(20) You are a doctor with five patients on life support, in need of transplants of various organs. A perfectly healthy patient comes in for a checkup. You could save the five patients by transplanting various of the new patient's organs into them. He will die if you do so, and the others will die if you do not.

As many have noted, cases like this one are not really specific: they plausibly elicit judgments about the *type* of situation described.

By contrast, we can make ethical judgments about completely specific actions. For example, consider:

(21) The US executive branch acted wrongly in authorizing the use of waterboarding and other techniques of interrogational torture during the so-called war on terror.

One fact about the practice of ethics is that, when judgments about cases like (20) conflict with judgments about general principles like (19), many philosophers tend to find judgments about cases more probative. This might seem to be some evidence for the idea that propositions about these cases are the propositions that are epistemically basic, or that in any case they tend to be better epistemically justified than highly general propositions.

Defenders of the relative epistemic credibility of general propositions have replied in at least two ways. First, they have argued that general propositions have epistemically important properties that specific propositions lack (e.g. Sidgwick 1981 [1907]), or at least that there is no clear rationale for prioritizing judgments about cases (Kagan 2001). Second, they have argued that judgments about cases are more vulnerable than judgments about abstract principles to some of the sorts of defeaters we discussed in Section 2 (Huemer 2008).

The question of relative epistemic credibility is *different* from the question of relative epistemic basicness: two claims could be equally basic, but one could be much better justified than the other. If only certain ethical claims are epistemically basic, then in explaining how ethical knowledge is possible, we need to understand how knowledge of *those* claims is possible. However, if certain ethical claims are much more credible than others, this might be a striking fact about what is epistemically distinctive of ethics that the epistemologist of ethics should try to explain.

Here, it is worth clarifying that *distinctive* features of the epistemology of ethics need not be *unique* to ethics. Various of the candidate features of the epistemology of ethics explored below may be shared by various other sorts of inquiry, such as philosophical inquiry more generally, aesthetic inquiry, or mathematical inquiry. With these clarifications in hand, we are ready to consider hypotheses about how ethical knowledge is possible.

4.2 Empirical Sources for Ethical Knowledge?

I organize this section and the next around the contrast between empirical and a priori justification. There is a long history in epistemology of distinguishing claims that we can come to know only by appeal to evidence provided by our senses, and claims that – at least in principle – we can come to know independently of our senses. For example, many philosophers have thought that we could know the following claims without evidence from our senses:

(22) 1+1=2
(23) No bachelors are married.
(24) Every thing is identical to itself.

Knowledge or justification for a claim that is independent of our senses is traditionally called *a priori* knowledge or justification. By contrast, knowledge or justification for a claim that depends on the evidence provided by our senses is called *a posteriori* or *empirical* knowledge or justification.[45]

In order for the idea of a priori knowledge to be plausible we need to distinguish the *evidential* role of our senses from other roles, which are typically treated as being compatible with a priori knowledge. Consider three examples. First, for creatures like us, sense experience is, in fact, a necessary condition on our being able to engage in reasoning at all. It is not clear that a person raised from birth in a sensory deprivation tank would be able to have much of a mental life at all. Second, sense experience is often the way that we acquire the concepts needed to understand claims. For example, one probably needs experience to acquire the concept MARRIAGE, which is needed to understand (23). Third, many apparently a priori claims are first learned empirically. For example, parents regularly teach children that 1+1=2. In each of these cases, experience plays an important role in enabling us to have the relevant knowledge. Epistemologists typically suggest that even if we needed experience to acquire the concepts and capacities to even think about a claim, and even if we in fact learned the claim empirically, the claim could be a priori if (possessing the concepts and capacities) we *can* verify that it is true just by thinking carefully about it.

This section considers the idea that we can have ethical knowledge from empirical sources. This idea can be motivated by considering cases:

(25) You see some hoodlums pour gasoline on a cat and ignite it. You can see that what they are doing is wrong (cf. Harman 1977: 4).
(26) Alice believes that homosexuality is wrong. Then, on the basis of the experience of coming to know a gay couple, Alice gradually comes to know that homosexuality is not wrong (McGrath 2004: 224–25).

---

[45] For an introduction to the idea of a priori knowledge, see Russell (2017). For important worries about the philosophical significance of the a priori/a posteriori distinction, see Williamson (2007).

In these cases, it appears that perceptual experience can give us new ethical knowledge. Despite the apparent plausibility of these cases, the idea that we can have ethical knowledge by perception faces important objections. Consider two examples.

The first objection denies that ethical properties can feature in the contents of perception. It might seem that only some things can be part of the content of perception. For example, I can see that you are red in the face, but I arguably can't just *see* that you have high blood pressure. The objector thinks that ethical properties are like having high blood pressure in this respect. Suppose we stumble upon some hoodlums burning a cat. If I didn't notice that the cat was on fire, you may wonder if I need new glasses. If I noticed them burning the cat, but didn't notice that anything wrong was happening, you will naturally worry about my character, not my eyes.[46]

The proponent of ethical knowledge by perception can potentially grant this objection. This is because we might have our ethical knowledge empirically, even if we cannot directly observe ethical properties. To see this, consider an analogy: even if I cannot directly see or hear your high blood pressure, my knowledge of facts about blood pressure is surely empirical. It is *indirect* empirical knowledge, mediated by a background theory that links what we can observe to facts about blood pressure. The proponent of ethical knowledge by perception can suggest a parallel structure for ethical knowledge.

The second sort of objection to a perceptual epistemology of ethics cuts more deeply. It argues that *even if* ethical perception is possible, it cannot explain how we get ethical knowledge. The idea is that ethical perception may turn out to be epistemically non-fundamental, in the way that testimony is. In both cases we may have a source of ethical knowledge, but it is one which only works if we have some other source of ethical knowledge to depend upon.

Here is the idea: it may sometimes be that knowledge is mediated by background theory (as in the blood pressure example), *even if* it is directly perceptual. Consider an example. I look out my window and see a pine tree. What makes it possible that my perceptual experience includes a *pine tree*, and not just a complicated arrangement of green and brown stuff? Presumably I have some background knowledge of what pine trees are, which informs my experience. My ability to have perceptual knowledge of pine trees is mediated by background knowledge about pine trees.

---

[46] For a defense of ethical contents in perception, see, for example, Cowan (2015). For a critique, see, for example, Vayrynen (2018).

A similar hypothesis seems plausible in the ethical case: even if I literally see that the cat burning is wrong, this must be because I already have some background ethical knowledge that informs my experience. In the case we imagined above, where I saw the cat burning but didn't see anything wrong, it is plausible that I was lacking precisely this background knowledge. However, if this is true for every ethical perception, then it appears that I must have acquired my ethical background by something other than ethical perception.[47] If so, ethical perception cannot be the answer to the "how is ethical knowledge possible?" question.

One might worry that this objection overgeneralizes. After all, my visual perception of objects in my environment is mediated, too, by my having a well-functioning visual system. In reply, the proponent of the objection might appeal to an allegedly deeper explanatory asymmetry: our perceptual system has been shaped by an evolutionary process that selected for the accuracy of this perceptual system (alongside efficiency and other "design constraints.") By contrast, it is at least initially hard to see how our ethical sensibility could have been "designed" for ethical accuracy. (Astute readers will note a connection to the skeptical argument from the genesis of our ethical beliefs in Section 2.) If this objection is sound, then one way that the epistemology of ethics might be distinctive is that ethical perception is necessarily epistemically superficial, in the sense explained.

Consider a different lesson to draw from cases like (25). Confronted with the cat burning, it would be natural to *feel horrified*. And we can easily imagine this feeling causing your belief that the hoodlums are acting wrongly. One sort of empiricist epistemology for ethics appeals to the idea that these feelings can themselves be evidence: that they can not only cause ethical beliefs, but also justify them.[48] If so, this might be a distinctive feature of the epistemology for ethics. For our feelings do not typically justify; I might "feel lucky" in a way that causes me to believe that I am going to be successful at some activity, but it is far from clear that this *justifies* my belief that I will succeed.

Despite these possibilities, it is common to think that the empiricist approaches just discussed are deeply misguided. The best sort of inquiry into basic ethical claims seems to many philosophers to be more a matter of careful thinking than of observation or feeling. I thus turn now to consider the idea that the epistemology of fundamental ethical claims is *a priori*.

---

[47] For this line of criticism, see Faraci (2015).

[48] See, for example, Johnston (2001); see Kauppinen (2018: ch. 5) for introduction to different ways to implement the idea.

4.3 A Priori Sources for Ethical Knowledge?

In this section, I consider three approaches to the idea that ethical knowledge is possible via a priori means. These are appeals to analyticity, to the alleged epistemic role of seemings states, and to the epistemic role of self-evidence.

It is traditional (although highly controversial) to distinguish between a priori knowledge that is based purely on our grasp of the meanings of our words or concepts (knowledge of "analytic" truths), and a priori knowledge that is not (knowledge of "synthetic" truths). Although I will now frame my discussion in terms of this distinction, it is worth noting that the existence of a genuine analytic/synthetic distinction is highly controversial.[49] Among those who accept the distinction, certain a priori claims are widely accepted to be analytic (for example, "No bachelor is married.") The possibility of synthetic a priori knowledge is more controversial still. Those who accept the possibility of the synthetic a priori have suggested as examples the truths of geometry, or examples like "No surface can be wholly colored red and wholly colored blue at the same time."

One might think of analyticity as potentially *explaining* the possibility of a priori knowledge. For example, one might think that we in general know the meanings of our own words a priori. And if we suppose that I know that 'bachelor' means 'adult unmarried male,' then it seems that we can explain how I can justifiably conclude that 'No bachelor is married' is true.

If there are analytic truths, it is plausible that some ethical truths are analytic: 'Murder is wrong' is a strong candidate, given that 'murder' just means something like wrongful killing. However, this sort of ethical knowledge may appear to some extent trivial. And a prominent tradition in ethics denies that we can appeal to analyticity to learn less trivial ethical truths. This denial can be motivated by noting that a mark of paradigmatic analytic truths is that their denial is evidence of confusion or conceptual incompetence. For example, if I deny that 'No bachelor is married' is true, this strongly suggests I may be confused or using words in a non-standard sense. By contrast, recall:

(17) It is (*at least* a little bit) bad to violently assault random strangers on a daily basis.

As obvious as (17) is, many people think that one could deny it without betraying confusion or incompetence with ethical language. The truth of (17)

---

[49] Complicating things further, there is more than a passing resemblance between the self-evidence account of a priority, discussed below, and the influential *epistemological* conception of analyticity (e.g. Boghossian 1996).

is, in G. E. Moore's vexed terminology, an "open question."[50] However we should ultimately understand this idea, it does seem to be picking out some relevant contrast between 'No bachelor is married' and (17). Some philosophers argue that despite this apparent contrast with paradigms of analytic truth, ethical claims like (17) can be analytic or "conceptual" truths (e.g. Jackson and Pettit 1995; Cuneo and Shafer-Landau 2014).

Suppose there can be a priori justification of ethical claims that is not a matter of knowing analytic truths. What, then, is the nature of this a priori justification? A very common contemporary answer to this question is that we can have knowledge of ethical claims by appeal to *intuitions*. A wide variety of views about ethics travel under the name "intuitionism." Here I will introduce two prominent and contrasting varieties of epistemic intuitionism about ethics.[51]

The first view begins with the idea that there is a distinctive class of mental states – intuitions – that have a distinctive epistemic significance. On the most influential version of this sort of intuitionism, intuitions are *intellectual seemings states*: states in which a proposition *seems true* to the bearer of the state. These states are distinct from beliefs, because a claim can *seem* true even if one doesn't believe it, and vice versa. For example, each of the premises in a paradox may seem true to me, even if I decline to believe any of them, because I know that they jointly entail a contradiction. Intellectual seemings are often claimed to be distinct from perceptual states but analogous to them: when I look at the wall, it (visually) seems beige to me. When I think about claim (17), it (intellectually) seems true to me. Some philosophers have suggested that this shared nature explains the justificatory role of seemings (e.g. Huemer 2007, Bengson 2015).

A very different view that is also called "intuitionism" claims that some propositions bear a distinctive epistemic property: they are *self-evident*. To warm up to this idea, recall:

(24) Every thing is identical to itself.

Focus on the *idea* or *proposition* expressed by (24). (Notice that the very same idea or proposition could be stated by a sentence in another language.) You might think that this proposition has the following property: adequately understanding it is sufficient to provide justification to believe it. Call propositions with this property *self-evident*. Many true propositions are not self-evident. For example, I can perfectly understand the proposition that Neela owns a cat without having any justification for believing it.

---

[50] Moore (1993 [1903]). See McPherson (2015c) for an introductory discussion.

[51] For a helpful introduction to intuitionism in the epistemology of ethics see Bedke (2010).

Some philosophers have thought that an important class of ethical claims are also self-evident (e.g. Sidgwick 1981 [1907]; Ross 2002 [1930]; Audi 2004). One virtue of the idea of self-evidence is that it potentially explains the possibility of ethical knowledge in terms of a completely general epistemic capacity. It may seem plausible that across a wide variety of topics, we need the ability to recognize truths that are self-evident. For example, many simple logical truths appear to be self-evident. And we might think that it is in general adaptive for a creature to be equipped with a reliable capacity to recognize self-evident truths. So our ethical reliability might be explained by our ability to exercise this general capacity.

The "open question" challenge mentioned above provides one initial challenge to the idea of ethical self-evidence. The truth of (24), like that of 'No bachelors are married,' is *not* an open question: its apparent sincere and thoughtful denial will tend to suggest confusion. By contrast, many fundamental ethical claims have been subject to persistent controversy among thoughtful, careful, and persistent inquirers. It is puzzling why a class of self-evident truths would be subject to such controversy. Absent special explanation, one would expect a self-evident truth to be, well, *evident* to an intelligent and clearheaded person who carefully considers it.

Notice a striking contrast between the intellectual seemings view and the self-evidence view. Self-evidence is a property of propositions, and not their relationships to particular individuals. So presumably a proposition cannot be self-evidently true "to me" and self-evidently false "to you." By contrast, intellectually seeming true is a relationship between a proposition and an individual's psychology. Just as – in tricky light – something red can seem brown, it is presumably possible for *any* ethical proposition to seem true to some particular thinker. For example, while claim (17) seems obviously true to me, it could potentially seem false to someone else.

In short, on the seemings view, different people can have different levels of a priori justification for the same ethical truth, but on the self-evidence view, all a priori ethical truths are equally justified for every believer. It is unclear which of these implications is more plausible. Suppose that some mathematical falsehood strikes me as true when I reflect on it. Do I thereby have a priori justification for believing it? One reason to say "yes" is that some mathematical and set-theoretic falsehoods have seemed true to many gifted inquirers. If these seemings can justify, this can potentially explain why such inquirers were reasonable when they formed beliefs on the basis of such seemings. One reason to say "no" is that it is hard to believe that I could be justified in believing that 1+1=3, for example, simply because it seemed true to me.

The self-evidence view prompts important questions about which ethical propositions are self-evident. For example, are all true ethical propositions self-evident or entailed by the self-evident (perhaps together with relevant empirical information, as in the example of the abrasive boss in Section 4.1)? If so, then the self-evidence view suggests that all ethical truths are knowable, at least in principle. It may seem plausible that some ethical truths are *not* knowable by appeal to the self-evident. If so, then either such truths are unknowable, or we need some other explanation of how knowledge of such truths is possible.

4.4 Is Ethical Testimony Distinctively Problematic?

In Section 4.1, I argued that we cannot explain how ethical knowledge is possible by appeal to ethical testimony. However, many philosophers have thought that testimony nonetheless teaches us something important about the epistemology of ethics. In a host of cases, from chemistry to cooking, deferring to experts in one's beliefs and actions typically seems untroubling, provided that one's confidence in the relevant expertise is warranted. Many philosophers have thought that ethics is different. These "pessimists" about ethical testimony think that there *is* something troubling about simply deferring to someone else concerning whether abortion is wrong, for example, rather than trying to think the matter through oneself (Wolff 1970; Hopkins 2007; Hills 2009; McGrath 2011).

It is controversial both *how much* ethical testimony is problematic and whether the relevant problem is epistemic in nature. Consider first the question of scope, in light of a pair of contrasting examples. Seeking testimony about whether it is wrong to torture a puppy appears both bizarre and worrying. By contrast, suppose that I know that my friend is much better able to identify wrongful sexist behavior than I am. On that basis, it seems wholly reasonable and appropriate for me to defer to their ethical judgment in identifying cases of such behavior (compare Jones 1999).

It is also controversial whether the problem with ethical testimony is epistemic at all. As several philosophers have noted, it is very plausible that we can have epistemically justified ethical belief on the basis of testimony (e.g. Jones 1999; Sliwa 2012). Contemporary pessimists typically grant this point, and argue for subtler connections. For example, perhaps we should strive to regulate our ethical opinions *autonomously* (Wolff 1970), or to hold ethical beliefs solely for the (ethical) reasons that *make them true* (Hopkins 2007), or perhaps ethical believers should aim at *understanding* rather than knowledge or truth (Hills 2009).

Each of the theses just mentioned is more straightforwardly motivated as a view about *ethically virtuous* cultivation of our ethical beliefs than as an *epistemic* norm. However, if we assume that the epistemology of ethics is in some way fitted to the virtuous agent, these ideas might nonetheless have epistemic implications.[52]

Any way of attempting to draw such epistemic implications will be controversial. But here is one idea: our epistemic practices in ethics seem to emphasize the importance of *explanatory intelligibility*, in a way that is not true everywhere. For example, philosophers like Judith Thomson who appeal to vivid examples like the transplant case (introduced in Section 4.1 above) do not stop after offering such cases. Instead, they typically go on to offer candidate explanations of the conclusions that they draw about the cases. This is not only true of professionals. Psychologists have studied the phenomenon of *moral dumbfounding*: they find cases where participants have a strong ethical reaction to a case, without an easily available explanation of why that reaction could be correct. In many such cases, participants appear to confabulate explanations that would vindicate their judgments, often contradicting elements of the cases they were presented in order to do so (Haidt 2001; for dissent see Royzman, Kim, and Leeman 2015).

The apparent importance of explanatory intelligibility may explain another seemingly distinctive feature of the epistemology of ethics. In epistemology generally, there is a controversy between *internalists* and *externalists* about epistemic justification. Very roughly, the internalist claims that justification is solely a matter of what is "in the head" of the agent, while the externalist claims that certain facts about one's environment can partly ground facts about epistemic justification. With only a few exceptions (e.g. Shafer-Landau 2003: ch. 12, Star 2008), the literature in the epistemology of ethics often appears to take for granted internalism about the epistemology of ethics. This may be partly explained by the idea that a preeminent aim of our epistemic practices in ethics is to make ethical explanations available to the agent.

Suppose that these aspects of common practice in the epistemology of ethics are on track: that explanatory intelligibility is epistemically important in ethics in a way that it is not in other domains. This might help to explain how the alleged defect in certain cases of accepting ethical testimony is epistemic, and not merely ethical in nature.

4.5 How Deeply Epistemically Distinctive Is Ethics?

I conclude this section by asking how we might explain the distinctive epistemic character of ethics. Suppose, for example, that explanatory intelligibility plays

---

[52] This paragraph draws on Fritz and McPherson (2019).

a distinctive role in the epistemology of ethics. How might this distinctive fact be explained?

At several points I have at least tacitly assumed what I will call the *epistemic continuity* picture. On this attractive picture, facts about the epistemology of ethics are ultimately explained by the interaction of (i) the correct general epistemic theory, together with (ii) the correct metaethical theory, which illuminates the nature of the subject matter of ethics. Consider a simplistic analogy to illustrate how this sort of unified explanation of diverse epistemic facts is possible. We could begin with a unified theory of memory as a source of epistemic justification, where causation played a role in the account of memory. Such a theory, together with facts about the relationship between causation and time, can plausibly explain why memory can justify beliefs about the past but not – at least directly – beliefs about the future.

If this epistemic continuity picture is correct, then there is reason to think that the epistemologist of ethics should be deeply interested in central questions in general epistemology, for just the same reason she should be interested in metaethical questions: because answers to these questions could potentially help us to discover or explain facts in the epistemology of ethics.[53]

As attractive as the epistemic continuity picture is, it is worth noting that it is not forced upon us. On an alternative *deep epistemic discontinuity* picture, the epistemic might be disunified "all the way down." That is, there might be distinctive facts about the epistemology of ethics that are not grounded in the application of a unified general epistemic theory to the ethical subject matter.

This sort of epistemic discontinuity picture has clear dangers of being ad hoc and explanatorily baffling: we would need to have a disjunctive story about the nature of epistemic relations like justification or knowledge. But some philosophers might be tempted to endorse epistemic discontinuity if doing so was the most elegant way to vindicate the distinctive epistemic character of ethics.

I closed Section 3 by proposing that the plausibility of metaethical theories rested in part on their ability to capture the distinctive epistemic character of ethics. As we have seen in this section, this task is complicated by a great deal of controversy concerning that epistemic character and its explanation.

5 Methodology in Ethics beyond Epistemology

The core methodological question about ethics is: how shall we go about investigating and answering ethical questions? Many of the epistemic questions

---

[53] For an excellent, if slightly dated introduction to general epistemology, see Feldman (2003).

that we have focused on in this Element so far are highly relevant to addressing the methodological question. Consider three brief examples. First, much of Section 4 concerned the search for sources of ethical knowledge. Identifying such sources of ethical knowledge is a natural step in ethical inquiry. Second, a central lesson of Section 3 was that metaethics and the epistemology of ethics have potentially powerful implications for each other. This might suggest that the methodologist of ethics has strong reasons to investigate metaethical questions as well (compare McPherson 2012). Third, the skeptical arguments discussed in Section 2 might inform the methodology of ethics in a different way. For if epistemic goals such as knowledge were unattainable, this would naturally motivate a methodology in ethics that abandoned epistemic goals in favor of some alternative.

More detailed discussion of such connections between the epistemology and methodology of ethics is clearly possible. However, for want of space, I will leave this part of the methodology of ethics to the reader. Instead, this section will focus on two central methodological questions about ethics that are largely independent of the epistemology of ethics:

The conceptual ethics question: *which words and concepts* should one use in ethical inquiry?

The goal question: *what counts as success* in one's inquiry about an ethical question?

These questions have tended to be neglected in the methodology of ethics. I will explain why they deserve serious attention.

The most prominent methodological proposal in ethics in the last half-century has been John Rawls' method of reflective equilibrium. I conclude the section by briefly explaining why this method is (at best) of extremely limited use in addressing the pressing methodological questions faced by ethical inquirers.

5.1 The Conceptual Ethics Question[54]

In ethical inquiry, we inevitably use words and concepts to frame our questions and to state and evaluate answers to those questions. It seems possible that certain words or concepts might be *better* to use than others, in our inquiry. This leads to a natural methodological question: which words and concepts should we use in this context? This is a question of *conceptual ethics*.[55]

---

[54] This section draws significantly on McPherson and Plunkett, (2020).
[55] For a general introduction to conceptual ethics, see Burgess and Plunkett (2013).

There are many questions in conceptual ethics. For example, we can ask *deontic* or *evaluative* questions about concept choice. We can ask questions about the role of certain non-ethical concepts in ethical inquiry. And we can ask questions about both *words* and *concepts*, and about the relationship between them. To keep this brief discussion manageable, I will narrow my focus to a single kind of question in conceptual ethics. This question is inspired by the idea that we can use different ethical concepts to fix contrasting topics for ethical inquiry. An inquiry about exploitation, for example, intuitively has a different topic than an inquiry about reasons for action. Here, I will focus on the following question: what broadly ethical concept(s) should we use to fix the topic of our ethical inquiry?

One motive for asking this question is simply the range of possible topics for ethical inquiry. For example, even if we focus on a specific agent in a completely determinate set of circumstances, normative inquirers can ask of that agent:

- what the agent *ought to do*, "all things considered"
- what it would be *prudent* for the agent to do
- what it would be *morally permissible* for the agent to do
- whether one of their options would constitute *exploitation*

This brief list of questions massively understates the range of topics we could investigate, for at least three reasons. First, there are many more existing ethical terms that one could use to frame one's ethical inquiry than were mentioned in the examples. Second, many existing ethical terms at least appear to be associated with strikingly different concepts. Consider, for example, the wide variety of ways that contemporary philosophers use the word 'rational.' Third, the ethical inquirer need not be restricted to our stock of *existing* ethical concepts. An analogy to scientific practice makes this clear: scientific practice continually involves both the refinement of existing concepts and the introduction of new ones.

On what basis should we select within this broad range of possible concepts? One possibility is that this is just a matter of individual interest. But it is also possible that we can make this choice on the basis of considerations that most ethical inquirers should care about. I frame my discussion around three such considerations: *normative authority*, *epistemic access*, and *defectiveness*. I introduce these considerations in turn.

First, as I suggested in Section 1, our normative concepts vary in how "weighty" or "important" they appear to be: moral concepts, for example, seem to be about *weightier* or *more authoritative* norms than chess concepts. Further, it is not obvious that MORAL is the *most* authoritative concept.

If morality and prudence conflict, for example, it is controversial which we *ought* to follow, in a presumptively authoritative sense of 'ought' (cf. McPherson 2018a).

If norms can in fact vary in authoritativeness, it is natural to think that it would be better to investigate more rather than less authoritative norms. Ethical inquiry, like any inquiry, can be motivated by the desire to know (or better understand, etc.) facts about our world. However, it is very natural to think that ethical inquiry can also be motivated by the desire to discover answers that can (in some sense) *directly* guide our decisions about how to live. And the more authoritative a concept is, the more significant are conclusions framed using that concept for questions concerning how to live.

Second, we arguably have *better epistemic access* to claims framed using certain ethical concepts than claims framed with others. To see this, consider controversy about which actions are morally wrong. You might think that, even if such controversy does not form the basis for a sound skeptical argument, it is a mark of the difficulty of finding knowledge about wrongness. You might think that there is much *less* reasonable controversy about which actions are *exploitative* or *prudent.* For example, suppose that you rescue a drowning person only on the condition that they then provide you with some large benefit. There is room for argument about whether this is morally wrong. By contrast, someone who denies that this is exploitation appears to lack a clear grip on the concept. And (if we make natural further assumptions about the case) it may also be clear whether demanding the benefit as a condition on rescue is *prudent.* There is a natural reason for focusing our ethical inquiry around questions to which we have better epistemic access: by doing so, we can hope to make it more likely that we achieve epistemic goods with that inquiry.

Third, some of our ethical concepts might be *defective* in one of two ways. On the one hand, they might be defective in leading our inquiry to misrepresent the world. (Compare organizing inquiry into physics around the concepts PHLOGISTON or ETHER.) On the other, they might be defective in a broader sense of being positively bad to use. Consider, for example, Marxist or Nietzschean hypotheses about the function of moral concepts: that they serve to make us willing accomplices of the capitalist class, or of the "herd." Or consider G. E. M. Anscombe's idea that our existing deontic concepts ought to be jettisoned, because they are "survivals" from a previous conception of ethics, and are "harmful" when divorced from that conception (1958: 1).

With such considerations in mind, an important question is: should we select among our existing stock of ethical concepts, or instead attempt to engineer new ethical concepts? One could argue for engineering ethical concepts on all three of the bases we have just introduced. First, it is not obvious that our existing concepts are the most authoritative. This raises an interesting kind of challenge to ethical inquiry-as-usual. For example, even if we can determine what we morally ought to do, applying this knowledge might only lead us away from what the most authoritative possible norms would require of us (cf. Eklund 2017: 14–15). If we can introduce an ethical concept that is transparently maximally authoritative, this would avoid the challenge. Second, we might hope that we could engineer concepts that give us better epistemic access to ethics. For example, in scientific inquiry, introducing concepts like ELECTRON and QUARK have allowed us to more aptly describe the subject matter being investigated. And other introduced concepts have been epistemically valuable in virtue of having precise and explicit content. Finally, we might be prompted to engineer by arguments that central existing ethical concepts are defective.

One could also potentially defend orienting inquiry around existing concepts on all three of these bases. First, it may be implausible that the most authoritative concepts do not show up in our lexicon; perhaps normativity could not be so detached from our ordinary practices. Second, our central existing concepts are arguably repositories of collective ethical *wisdom* in the sense of giving us epistemic access to relatively authoritative norms. It is much less clear how one could introduce a concept that was both authoritative and which put us in a good position to identify or investigate its extension. Finally, as the controversy around the defectiveness of our existing concepts shows, the defectiveness of a concept is not a transparent matter. And we have at least had time to identify defects in our existing concepts. We might worry that important defects in engineered concepts might be hard to discover.

I have framed this section around three considerations that I suggested that ethical inquirers should care about: *normative authority, epistemic access*, and *defectiveness*. One might note, however, that the broad question raised in this section – What concept(s) *should* we use to fix the topic of our ethical inquiry? – is itself a seemingly ethical question. To engage in conceptual ethics is to deploy normative concepts. And of course, the question of conceptual ethics applies to these concepts as well: what normative concept(s) should we use in raising this question? To use our existing normative concepts leaves open the possibility that our concepts are somehow flawed; to use introduced concepts seemingly requires that we have already determined how to evaluate these introduced concepts. A regress evidently threatens.[56] Instead of taking up this vexed issue, I will instead turn to the second methodological question.

---

[56] See Burgess (2020) and McPherson and Plunkett (forthcoming) for relevant discussion.

5.2 The Goal Question[57]

Suppose that you have settled on an ethical question to investigate. For example: the question of whether or not it is morally wrong to eat meat. A further methodological question is: what should your *goal* be in this inquiry? What should count as answering this question *successfully*? (I will treat these as equivalent.)

It is comparatively uncommon for philosophers investigating ethical questions to explicitly broach the goal question. Perhaps this is because it is taken to be common knowledge that we typically approach ethical inquiry with a certain goal in mind. But even if this is so, it would not settle the goal question: for the methodologist can ask whether we could do better in some significant respect by adopting an alternative to the commonly accepted goal.

Let us make things more concrete with an example. It might seem that the obvious answer to the goal question is also the best one: if you are investigating a question – including an ethical question – your activity should count as successful just in case your answer to that question is *true*. This may be an excellent answer in many cases. But it faces important challenges and competitors.

We can begin by asking *why* we should accept the truth goal. We can see the force of this challenge by considering a natural reply to this question. This is that we should pursue truth in our inquiry because truth is a *constitutive* goal of ethical inquiry. The idea of a constitutive goal is familiar. For example, if you are taking turns moving chess pieces around with your friend, but in no way trying to deliver checkmate or otherwise win, you are arguably not playing chess. This is because trying to win is arguably part of what it is to play chess; it is a *constitutive goal* for the activity. One might propose that trying to identify the true answer to your question is constitutive of inquiry into a question. If so, failing to aim at truth disqualifies one from counting as engaging in ethical *inquiry*.

The difficulty with this constitutivist explanation of why truth is the goal of inquiry is that it does not explain why I should care about whether I am engaged in inquiry *strictly speaking*. Suppose that I can engage in something very much like ethical inquiry, but which has a slightly different constitutive goal. Then, instead of asking why we should take truth to be the goal of our inquiry, we can simply ask: what goals should we have in our inquiry-ish activity that addresses ethical questions?[58] In light of this sort of challenge to the idea that there is an easy answer to the goal question, I will assume that there are substantive

---

[57] This sections draws significantly on unpublished work coauthored with David Plunkett.
[58] Compare Enoch (2006) for this sort of objection to appeals to constitutive goals.

methodological questions about what goals we should have in normative inquiry.

In asking what goals we should have in ethical inquiry, it will be useful to distinguish *proximate* from *ultimate* goals. This distinction can be illustrated by two oft-cited goals for *believing,* relative to a proposition P:

(i) The goal of believing the truth concerning whether P
(ii) The goal of apportioning your beliefs to your evidence concerning P

These goals are distinct: because one's evidence is sometimes incomplete or misleading, one can achieve one of these goals without achieving the other. Take a simple example: suppose that a trusted friend misleads you about P. Your friend's testimony may be sufficient evidence that justifies believing that P. So believing that P will accomplish goal (ii) here. But because this testimony is in fact misleading, believing that P will fail to achieve goal (i).

Next, consider why one might adopt goal (ii). One might do so because one has a special fetish for evidence. But many of us will seek to apportion our beliefs to our evidence because we think this is a good strategy for trying to acquire true beliefs. In doing so, we treat goal (ii) as a *proximate goal*, which we adopt as a way to achieve a more *ultimate* goal: believing truly. My point here is not to endorse this idea about goals for believing, but rather to use it to orient readers to the distinction between proximate and ultimate goals for inquiry.[59] I structure the following discussion around this distinction.

5.2.1 Ultimate Goals for Ethical Inquiry

In thinking about ultimate goals for ethical inquiry, it is useful to ask whether we should conceive of these goals *individualistically* or *collectivistically.* To see this distinction, imagine that I bake an inedible, cake-shaped disaster, and this prompts you to bake a delicious cake to share with me. Has my activity succeeded or failed? If my goal in baking is that *I produce* a delicious cake, I have failed. However, if my goal is that *we wind up with* a delicious cake, then we have succeeded. We can think of the first goal as individualistic and the second as collective. Further, if I have the collective goal, I can even take my own baking to have contributed to the goal. After all, my failed baking contributed importantly to our achieving the collective goal, by motivating you to bake the delicious cake.

For many socially structured inquiries, it is plausible that it makes sense for participants to orient themselves toward *collective* rather than *individualistic*

---

[59] Copp (2012) is an important example of use of the proximate/ultimate goal distinction in the methodology of ethics and political philosophy.

epistemic goals. For example, if Sarai simply wants to know as much physics as possible, she should not dedicate her time to constructing experiments; it would be much more efficient to simply voraciously read others' work. However, by conducting experiments, Sarai can hope to contribute to the collective effort to advance the frontiers of our knowledge of physics. If we think of ethical inquiry as a collective epistemic project, then it may make sense for the individual ethical inquirer to think of their goal in similar terms, as *contributing to advancing the frontiers of ethical knowledge*.[60]

A salient possibility already mentioned is that our ultimate goal in ethical inquiry should simply be truth, understood as either a collective or an individualistic goal. Because this idea is so familiar, I will focus here on explaining important alternatives to this picture. I will first discuss *epistemic* alternatives to truth as a goal, before considering candidate *practical* goals for ethical inquiry.

One obvious candidate epistemic goal for ethical inquiry is *knowledge*. One rationale for this goal is suggested by the long history of philosophers arguing that knowledge is more valuable than true belief.[61] If this idea can be made out, then knowledge might be a better goal for inquiry, precisely because it is more valuable when attained.

Another important epistemic goal is *understanding*.[62] Such a goal plausibly structures much ethical inquiry. For example, many ethical theorists have explanatory ambitions: they are seeking to understand what makes acts right, not merely to know that this or that act is right. There are also more modest versions of this sort of ambition. Suppose one thought that one cannot know what fundamental account of moral rightness is correct. One might seek to show both that some candidate fundamental account of rightness is credible and that it *would* provide understanding of what makes acts morally right, if it *were* correct.

The question of whether we should take understanding as a goal – either as a complement or a competitor to truth or knowledge – can have significant implications for inquiry. For example, understanding and knowledge as goals can pull in very different directions in applied ethics. For example, consider:

(27) It is typically wrong to make an animal suffer.
(28) It is typically wrong for a doctor not to seek the consent of a competent patient before treating that patient.

---

[60] There are many important questions about what it would be for a collective to enter into epistemic relations like knowledge or justification. For an introduction see Goldman and Blanchard (2018: section 4).

[61] For an introduction to debates about the value of knowledge, see Pritchard, Turri, and Carter (2018).

[62] For defense of understanding as a goal of ethical inquiry, see Hills (2009).

These claims are both highly plausible. They can thus serve as important premises in compelling arguments in applied ethics. However, it is very unlikely that they are explanatorily fundamental. For example, an act–utilitarian, a Kantian deontologist, and a contractualist are likely to offer quite different explanations of why these claims are true. Now consider the choice between defending a thesis in applied ethics by appeal to claims like (27) or (28), on the one hand, or by appeal to a systematic normative ethical theory, on the other. If successful, the second strategy promises to provide deeper understanding of why the thesis being defended is true. However, theses like (27) and (28) are arguably significantly more credible than any such systematic ethical theory could be. So any attempt to provide deeper understanding of a question in applied ethics by appeal to such a theory will risk less reliably securing the truth than answering such a question by appeal to premises like (27) and (28). This means that adjudicating between pursuing the truth goal and the understanding goal is quite important for whether the inquirer should rest satisfied with premises like (27) or (28), or insist on attempting to ground their ethical conclusion in an explanatory normative ethical theory.

I now shift focus to views on which the ultimate goal of ethical inquiry is neither truth nor an epistemic property. Such alternatives can be initially motivated in at least three ways. First, as we have seen in Sections 2 and 3, our evidence might support (or at least prevent us from ruling out) a metaethical theory on which there are no ethical truths. Second, even if there are ethical truths, we have seen that there are powerful arguments that suggest that we are unable to constructively pursue truth or epistemic goals in ethics (such as the skeptical arguments considered in Section 2). To the extent that they are credible, these considerations suggest that the pursuit of truth in ethical inquiry might be *futile*, and this might encourage us to consider alternative goals.

Finally, ethical inquiry seems poised to make a practical difference in our lives. It is natural to think that as ethical inquirers, we should be concerned about the practical significance of our inquiry. Notice that this sort of concern seems relevant to our inquiry whether or not the pursuit of ethical truth is futile. For example, accepting or circulating ethical truths need not always have good effects. And where it does not, we could thus face a choice between accepting or circulating ethical claims that are true, or those whose acceptance or circulation would have good effects.

Consider a goal for ethical inquiry that might be motivated as a response to the futility worry. Even if we cannot attain epistemic goals in ethics, we might still feel the force of the criticism: *you wouldn't believe that if you really thought it through*. Plausibly, almost all of us have some tensions in our thinking, making some of our beliefs vulnerable to this sort of criticism. This sort of criticism is also potentially potent: it is hard to continue to believe something if you accept that you *wouldn't* believe it if you really thought it through. One goal that you might have for your ethical inquiry is to make this sort of criticism inapt for your ethical beliefs. That is, you might aim for your belief with respect to a claim to be stable, in a way that ensures that you would not be made to change your mind by fair-minded Socratic cross-examination. Call such a state *Socratic invulnerability*. Socratic invulnerability is a potentially appealing goal that could structure much of your ethical inquiry.

The remainder of this section will focus on characterizations of the ultimate goal of ethical inquiry that take the distinctive practical significance of ethical inquiry to structure the goals of such inquiry.[63] This idea is familiar from an important strand of social theory. For example, the work of the Frankfurt School and other influential proponents of critical theory can be read as oriented toward promoting human emancipation, or other political goals (compare Geuss 1981: 1–2). Or consider Sally Haslanger's pathbreaking work on categories like race and gender (e.g. 2012). As Haslanger emphasizes, much of this work is structured by the goal of promoting *social justice*. For example, she asks what properties broadly connected to "race" and "gender" it would be helpful to keep track of and study for the purposes of understanding and opposing our current circumstances of racial and gender injustice. Similar goals might be attractive in the context of ethical inquiry: it is natural to want one's ethical inquiry to promote social justice rather than to impair it.

Other practical goals for ethical inquiry might be *procedural*. That is, our ultimate goals for ethical inquiry might in part directly concern how that inquiry is conducted, as opposed to simply focusing on its results. Consider just one example of the many rich procedural questions to ask in evaluating the social organization of ethical inquiry. It is plausible that across its history, systematic ethical inquiry has typically taken place in institutional contexts that tend to systematically exclude or marginalize the voices of those most disadvantaged by prevailing ethical norms. One might think that procedural justice in ethical inquiry demands that this be corrected, so that the practice of ethical inquiry comes to prioritize or at least to include the voices of those most affected by acceptance of the sorts of ethical norms that the relevant inquiry explores.

Another class of candidate practical constraints on ethical inquiry can be identified by adapting ideas that are usually proposed instead as claims about the

---

[63] The broadly related idea that moral claims could be 'practically' justified in a way independent of their epistemic status is helpfully discussed in Copp (1991).

true ethical theory. I will discuss three examples: publicity constraints, inter-personal justifiability, and transcendental justifiability.

It is sometimes insisted that the correct moral principles will satisfy a publicity condition: that they will be such that, were they to become common knowledge, various good effects would occur, or, at least, certain disastrous effects would not.[64] Whether some such publicity condition is in fact true of morality rests on difficult moral and metamoral issues. By contrast, there are fairly obvious reasons for adopting a publicity constraint as a constraint on one's ethical inquiry, if one intends one's research to be made public. Many of these reasons are wholly independent of whether the publicity condition is true of morality. For example, as Henry Sidgwick imagines, the correct morality might be *esoteric*, in the sense of being best kept from public circulation and adoption (1981 [1907]: 489–90). And that same morality might call for the investigation and circulation of moral claims that satisfy a publicity condition.

Next, consider the condition of *being permitted by a set of rules that no one could reasonably reject*. Some contractualists think that this or a similar condition is central to the correct foundational explanation of morality (e.g. Scanlon 1998). Roughly, on this sort of view, what it is for an action to be morally permissible is just for that action to satisfy the contractualist condition. This proposal is again highly controversial. But notice that even if one were agnostic about the truth of contractualism, it would be independently attractive to seek to identify ethical principles that satisfy this condition. For example, suppose that certain substantively decent social arrangements satisfied this condition, while others did not. And suppose that one was committed to achieving social change in ways that respect others' autonomy and liberty. It might be easier to bring about a substantively just social arrangement in ways that respected this commitment, if that arrangement satisfied the contractualist condition.

Finally, consider the condition of *being transcendentally justifiable*. Roughly, for a proposition to be transcendentally justifiable is for it to be the case that every agent is necessarily committed to this proposition, in light of its role in some inescapable project. Some philosophers have argued that such transcendental justification is the basis for ethical truth (e.g. Korsgaard 1996). However, we might accept that some ethical principles are transcendentally justifiable, without concluding that they must be true in virtue of this fact (compare Shah 2010: §I). Even if transcendental justifiability does not entail truth, identifying the transcendentally justifiable principles might be a very attractive goal for

---

[64] Compare Brandt (1992 [1965]: 136) and Hooker (2000: 85).

one's ethical theorizing. After all, if you managed to show that some ethical principle is transcendentally justifiable in this way, you would then be in a position to show your interlocutors that they are inescapably committed to this principle, and such a demonstration might be extremely practically important in any number of ways.

These examples bring out an important lesson: it *may* be that publicity or satisfaction of a contractual procedure or transcendental justifiability are built into the nature of certain ethical concepts or properties, such that they play a central role in explaining ethical truths. However, even if they are not, identifying principles with these features might be an important practical goal for ethical inquiry.

Finally, it is worth emphasizing that it may be appropriate to have multiple ultimate goals for ethical inquiry. For example, it might be appropriate to have both procedural goals and goals concerning the nature of the outcome of the inquiry.

5.2.2 Proximate Goals for Ethical Inquiry

In this section, I consider candidate *proximate* goals for ethical inquiry. As I mentioned when introducing this idea, a focus on proximate goals can be motivated by the thought that certain ultimate goals for ethical inquiry are not the sorts of things that we can effectively *follow*. I begin by sketching different ways of thinking about followability.

On one extreme, a norm is followable for me just in case trying to follow the norm guarantees successfully following it. On this *counterfactual success* standard, the norm of arithmetical addition is not followable in every case, since every human will make occasional mistakes in addition. On the other extreme, a norm is followable for me just in case it is *possible* for me to successfully follow it. The norm *believe any a priori truth that you consider and understand* is followable in this *possible success* sense, since every such truth is presumably possibly knowable by me. There is, of course, a range of more nuanced possible standards between these extremes.

How we think of followability matters. Consider the question: *what should you do when you are uncertain about fundamental ethical matters?* One might think the answer to this question depends on what ethical norms are followable. Suppose that the fundamental ethical truths are all a priori knowable by you. The possible success account of followability suggests the answer: do whatever you in fact ought to do. On the other hand, the counterfactual success standard might suggest an answer like: do whatever accords with the norm that seems to you most likely to be true.[65] (This is too simple; if

---

[65] For an introduction to central issues about decision making under ethical uncertainty, see Sepielli (2019).

one of my options has some risk of being ethically catastrophic, perhaps that should matter too.)

We have been considering questions about how to *act* given facts about the followability of ethical norms. A related question concerns how to conduct ethical *inquiry* if our ultimate goals are not directly followable. We saw above that one might think of the norm *apportion your beliefs to the evidence* as a proximate goal that serves the ultimate goal of believing truly. However, as the example of a priori truths just provided illustrates, the norm *apportion your beliefs to the evidence* may itself not be followable. This might inspire the search for yet more proximate goals.

To begin, I will show that some of the goals I have discussed as ultimate goals could also be naturally treated as proximate goals. Consider two examples. First, one could accept a proximate goal by appeal to *epistemic self-trust*. One rationale for such self-trust is that if one is going to inquire about a question at all, and one seeks the truth in such an inquiry, one *has* to think that one is capable of arriving at the truth.[66] If you embrace epistemic self-trust, you might embrace what I dubbed "Socratic invulnerability" in Section 5.2.1 as a *proximate* goal: trusting yourself, you might take Socratic invulnerability to be a good guide to truth.

Second, consider the idea of seeking to include the voices of those most affected by the sorts of norms that one's ethical inquiry addresses. One could endorse this as a procedural goal not because one thinks this makes the practice of inquiry more just, but because one thinks it will make that inquiry more *reliable*. This idea aligns with the core hypothesis of *standpoint epistemology:* that those persons disadvantaged by certain social phenomena will be more reliable with respect to those phenomena.[67] One might take this idea to extend to relevant ethical reliability. For example, one might think that those who suffer racial injustice will tend to be more reliable inquirers regarding questions of racial justice.

Next, consider two possible epistemic proximate goals for ethical inquiry.[68] Suppose that your ultimate goal is to identify the truth about the ethical questions you address, but that you take yourself to be unable to reliably achieve this goal. This might plausibly be the case if your ultimate goal is to identify the correct fundamental ethical theory. One appealing proximate goal for someone facing this sort of situation is to develop and defend a theory to such an extent that the central claims of that theory deserve a non-trivial proportion of our

---

[66] For discussions of epistemic self-trust, see Foley (2001: Part 1) and Zagzebski (2012: ch. 2).

[67] For introductory discussion see Anderson (2017, section 2).

[68] This paragraph and the next draw on McPherson (2018b).

credences. Or – if one is offering a novel defense of an existing thesis – to *increase* the credibility of that thesis by one's work.

One's proximate goals might be even more modest than this. One significant sort of philosophical progress consists in making the community of inquirers aware of interesting possibilities that we would not otherwise attend to. One's research might aim specifically to contribute to such progress, by investigating whether a certain thesis can be worked out in enough detail to illuminate an interesting and significant bit of "logical space."[69]

Finally, as I mentioned above, our ultimate goals might be collective: that *we* move forward the frontiers of knowledge on a given topic. A natural proximate goal for an individual given this ultimate goal is to *contribute* to the intellectual progress within the community as a whole. Such a proximate goal would help to vindicate activities such as presenting or publishing one's research. This is especially true for inquirers who write papers arguing for positions which they are either already highly confident in, or – conversely – offering a novel defense of positions that they find ultimately unattractive.

Conceiving of ethical inquiry as a collective social project might matter in a different way for our thinking about proximate goals. A familiar idea from the philosophy of science is that methodological diversity may help to promote successful inquiry. This may also be the case for proximate goals: the best overall social organization of ethical inquiry may involve different parts being organized around quite contrasting proximate goals. For example, perhaps it is useful to have some inquirers focused on clearly delineating the relevant "logical space" for fundamental ethical views, indifferent to its practical uses or consequences. And perhaps it is also useful for other inquirers to develop means of reasoning that can help communities of ordinary people to better solve the practical problems that face them.[70]

5.2.3 Interaction between Goals and Conceptual Ethics

So far in this section, I have treated the conceptual ethics question and the goal question separately. However, these questions interact in deep ways. For example, what goals it makes sense to have in ethical inquiry can inform which concepts it makes sense to deploy in that inquiry.

---

[69] One important metaethical example of theorizing that explicitly adopts this goal: Gibbard claims that the aim of much of his (2003) is not to defend expressivism as an interpretative thesis about actual ethical thought and talk, but rather to spell out how an expressivist theory *could* explain certain features of a system of recognizably ethical-ish thought and talk (e.g. 2003: 7–8).

[70] For a helpful characterization of the latter sort of methodology in ethics, which is also sensitive to issues of procedural justice, see Tobin and Jaggar (2013).

In the discussion of conceptual ethics, I focused on three potential bases for concept choice: authoritativeness, epistemic access, and defectiveness. The sorts of goals we discussed in the Section 5.2.2 can make a difference to how important each of these bases is. I will illustrate this in three ways. First, showing that an existing concept is defective in some way might seem like a clear reason to abandon it. But some philosophers have argued for retaining defective ethical concepts, because their use has good practical effects, even if their use leads us to misrepresent the world (e.g. Olson 2014: section 9.3).

Second, if one's ethical inquiry has an epistemic goal, it makes sense to be concerned with whether we can have good epistemic access to the extensions of the ethical concepts we deploy in that inquiry. However, if our inquiry has practical goals, we may be less concerned with this. For example, suppose our inquiry was structured around the goal of achieving transcendental or interpersonal justifiability for our conclusions. Such justifiability might be possible for claims using a concept, even if the truth of those claims was inaccessible to us.

Finally, notice that we might in effect embed a certain goal for ethical inquiry into a concept. For example, rather than thinking that we were engaged in inquiry concerning what we ought to do, where Socratic invulnerability was our goal in this inquiry, we might instead introduce a concept – the OUGHT OF SOCRATIC INVULNERABILITY – and frame our inquiry around what is true of that concept. In this way, an apparently distinctive *goal* of inquiry has been transformed into a constituent of the *content* of the inquiry. It is an interesting question what difference locating something in the content versus the goal of inquiry makes.

5.3 Reflective Equilibrium

Over the past half-century, the most influential methodological proposal in ethics has been John Rawls' method of reflective equilibrium. Two examples illustrate this influence. First, Michael Smith suggests that Rawls' account of the method successfully systematizes our methodological platitudes (1994: 40). Second, Shelly Kagan suggests that all practicing normative theorists are at least implicitly committed to something very similar to the method (1998: 16). And similar endorsements are remarkably common. Despite this, I have not yet discussed reflective equilibrium in this Element. This reflects my view that, despite their influence, Rawls' ideas about methodology are not helpful either as ways of framing central methodological questions about ethics, or as providing plausible answers to those questions. I will now explain why, by briefly explaining the most important elements of the method of reflective equilibrium, as canonically presented in Rawls' *A Theory of Justice* (1999b).

We can divide the method into two components. The first is an account of the *inputs* to be drawn on in moral and political theorizing, and the second is an account of the *operations* to be performed with those inputs. The central inputs to the method are what Rawls dubs "considered judgments": those judgments one sincerely and stably affirms in conditions which minimize the influence of strong emotion or self-interest (1999b: 42). The operations begin by formulating what one takes to be plausible moral principles, which purport to explain the ethical theses expressed by one's considered judgments. Because it is typically very difficult to find plausible principles that adequately explain the full range of one's considered judgments, the method then requires that one attempt to fit these judgments and principles into a coherent scheme. One does this by modifying, adding, or abandoning principles or particular judgments as one deems appropriate on reflection (1999b: 18). Finally, during this process, one is also supposed to take into consideration all plausible theories on the topic, and the reasonable arguments that can be made in support of each (cf. 1999b: 43).[71]

The account of inputs and operations might seem highly methodologically informative. But the final clause of the method eviscerates much of this informativeness. For it ensures that every possible reasonable argument on the topic – no matter the nature of its premises – is in effect an independent input to the method, relevant for consideration. What remains distinctive of the method is what determines the correct response to this panoply of inputs: one's own reflective judgment. This is both disappointing and implausible.

It is disappointing because one might have hoped that a methodology would have given one some *guidance* regarding this important methodological question, rather than instructing you to *do what strikes you as right*. It is implausible because sometimes inquirers will be disposed to respond to inputs in substantively irrational ways. To make this vivid, suppose that I am a juror. There is video of the defendant committing the crime, their fingerprints are on the weapon, etc. Suppose that I accept all of this evidence, but on reflection take it to support the conclusion that the defendant is innocent, because my belief-forming methods about this matter are deeply irrational. If we extended the method of reflective equilibrium to the determination of guilt and innocence, it would imply that I have proceeded appropriately here. But that is palpably

---

[71] Rawls later famously called an equilibrium formed after consideration of all such theories and arguments a "wide" reflective equilibrium (1999a).

absurd: no methodology should endorse paradigms of irrational ethical belief formation.[72]

One qualification to these objections is called for. Rawls' methodology is partly structured by an unusual answer to what I have called the goal question. He famously describes the goal of "moral theory" as being "at first" to describe our "moral capacity" or sensibility (1999b: 41). Rawls later clarified that in engaging in moral theory we "put aside the idea of constructing a correct theory of right and wrong" (1999a: 288). It is possible that taking the method of reflective equilibrium to address this goal might serve to vindicate the otherwise apparently objectionable features of this proposed methodology that I have identified. But it would also make pressing the question of what could be said in favor of adopting this proposed goal for ethical inquiry.

For these sorts of reasons, I doubt whether reflective equilibrium has a helpful role to play in the methodology of ethics. If I am mistaken about this, however, reflective equilibrium raises a host of interesting methodological questions. For example: what is the significance of reflective equilibrium for the skeptical arguments discussed in Section 2? Does it undercut those arguments or leave them untouched? What is the relationship between the role of considered judgments in the method and the questions broached in Section 4 about the *sources* of ethical knowledge?

6 Conclusions

Over the past fifteen years or so, inquiry into the epistemology and methodology of ethics has become one of the most vibrant and diverse areas of philosophy. My aim in this Element has been to put the reader in a position to navigate the broad structure of questions and topics inhabited by contemporary research and controversy in this area. The careful reader should now be in a position to understand and distinguish some of the major questions, positions, and arguments that make these topics so exciting.

One of the lessons I have sought to emphasize in this Element is that there are complex relationships among the different topics that constitute the epistemology and methodology of ethics. As we have seen, one compelling motivation for engaging in the epistemology of ethics is to understand and assess the threat of skepticism about ethical knowledge. I emphasized that how powerful that threat is depends in part on the nature of the correct metaethic. And the credibility of candidate metaethical theories depends in turn upon the plausibility of their implications for the epistemology of ethics. Similarly, it is plausible that

---

[72] For a more detailed exposition of related arguments against reflective equilibrium, see McPherson (2015b).

conclusions in the epistemology of ethics have a natural role to play in the methodology of ethical inquiry. (For example, our methodological situation will look very different if ethical knowledge is easy to acquire, or impossible.) But there are also reasons to think that practical goals matter for ethical inquiry in a way that they might not in other domains.

These connections are important, but they are often left implicit or obscure in papers in the epistemology or methodology of ethics. The astute reader can thus use the connections introduced and illustrated in this Element as critical tools when reading work in this area. My hope is that the Element will allow the astute reader to identify implicit assumptions about these connections (or their absence) that are doing important work in the background of much of this work. And I hope that this in turn helps put the reader in a position to make contributions that advance our collective understanding of these topics.

Bibliography

Alston, W. (2005). *Beyond "Justification."* Ithaca: Cornell University Press.

Anderson, E. (2017). Feminist Epistemology and Philosophy of Science. In E. Zalta, ed., *The Stanford Encyclopedia of Philosophy* (Spring 2017 Edition), https://plato.stanford.edu/archives/spr2017/entries/feminism-epistemology/.

Audi, R. (2004). *The Good in the Right*, Princeton: Princeton University Press.

Baker, D. (2018). The Varieties of Normativity. In T. McPherson & D. Plunkett, eds., *The Routledge Handbook of Metaethics*. New York: Routledge, 567–81.

Bedke, M. S. (2010). "Intuitional Epistemology in Ethics." *Philosophy Compass*, 5(12), 1069–83.

(2018). Cognitivism and Non-Cognitivism. In T. McPherson & D. Plunkett, eds., *The Routledge Handbook of Metaethics*. New York: Routledge, 292–307.

Bengson, J. (2015). "The Intellectual Given.' *Mind*, 124(495): 707–60.

Boghossian, P. (1996). "Analyticity Reconsidered." *Noûs*, 30(3): 360–91.

Bolinger, R. (2018). *The Rational Impermissibility of Accepting (Some) Racial Generalizations*. Synthese.

Brandt, R. (1992). *Morality, Utilitarianism, and Rights*, Cambridge: Cambridge University Press.

Burgess, A. (2020). Never Say "Never." In A. Burgess, H. Cappelan, & D. Plunkett, eds., *Conceptual Ethics and Conceptual Engineering*. Oxford: Oxford University Press, 125–131.

Burgess, A. & Plunkett, D. (2013). "Conceptual Ethics I." *Philosophy Compass*, 8(12): 1091–1101.

Caruso, G. (2018). Skepticism about Moral Responsibility. In E. Zalta, ed., *The Stanford Encyclopedia of Philosophy* (Spring 2018 Edition), https://plato.stanford.edu/archives/spr2018/entries/skepticism-moral-responsibility/.

Chignell, A. (2018). The Ethics of Belief. In E. Zalta, ed., *The Stanford Encyclopedia of Philosophy* (Spring 2018 Edition), https://plato.stanford.edu/archives/spr2018/entries/ethics-belief/.

Christensen, D. (2007). "Epistemology of Disagreement: The Good News." *The Philosophical Review*, 116(2): 187–217.

(2010). "Higher-Order Evidence." *Philosophy and Phenomenological Research*, 81(1): 185–215.

Cohen, S. (2016). "Theorizing about the Epistemic." *Inquiry*, 59(7–8): 839–57.

Copp, D. (1991). "Moral Skepticism." *Philosophical Studies*, 62(3): 203–33.

(2008). "Darwinian Skepticism about Moral Realism." *Philosophical Issues*, 18(1): 186–206.

(2012). Experiments, Intuitions, and Methodology in Moral and Political Theory. In R. S. Landau, ed., *Oxford Studies in Meta-Ethics*, vol. 7. Oxford: Oxford University Press, 1–36.

Cowan, R. (2015). "Perceptual Intuitionism." *Philosophy and Phenomenological Research*, 91(1), 164–93.

Cuneo, T.& Shafer-Landau, R. (2014). "The Moral Fixed Points." *Philosophical Studies*, 171(3): 399–443.

Darwall, S. (2018). Ethics and Morality. In T. McPherson & D. Plunkett, eds., *The Routledge Handbook of Metaethics*. New York: Routledge, 552–66.

Descartes, R. (1984). *Philosophical Writings Vol. 2.* J. Cottingham, R. Stoothoff, & D. Murdoch, trans. Cambridge: Cambridge University Press.

Dorr, C. (2002). "Non-Cognitivism and Wishful Thinking." *Noûs*, 36(1): 97–103.

Dunaway, W. (2018). Realism and Objectivity. In T. McPherson & D. Plunkett, eds., *The Routledge Handbook of Metaethics*. New York: Routledge, 135–50.

Eklund, M. (2017). *Choosing Normative Concepts*, Oxford: Oxford University Press.

Enoch, D. (2006). "Agency, Shmagency." *Philosophical Review*, 115(2): 169–98. (2011). *Taking Morality Seriously*. Oxford: Oxford University Press.

Faraci, D. (2015). "A Hard Look at Moral Perception." *Philosophical Studies*, 172(8): 2055–72.

Feldman, R. (2003). *Epistemology*. Upper Saddle River: Prentice Hall.

Fine, K. (2001). "The Question of Realism." *Philosophers' Imprint*, 1(1): 1–30.

Foley, R. (2001). *Intellectual Trust in Oneself and Others*. Cambridge: Cambridge University Press.

Fricker, M. (2007). *Epistemic Injustice*. Oxford: Oxford University Press.

Fritz, J. (2017). "Pragmatic Encroachment and Moral Encroachment." *Pacific Philosophical Quarterly*, 98(51), 643–61.

Fritz, J. & McPherson, T. (2019). "Moral Steadfastness and Meta-Ethics." *American Philosophical Quarterly*, 56(1): 43–55.

Geuss, R. (1981). *The Idea of a Critical Theory*. Cambridge: Cambridge University Press.

Gibbard, A. (2003). *Thinking How to Live*. Cambridge, MA: Harvard University Press.

Goldman, A. & Blanchard, T. (2018). Social Epistemology. In E. Zalta, ed., *The Stanford Encyclopedia of Philosophy* (Summer 2018 Edition), https://plato .stanford.edu/archives/sum2018/entries/epistemology-social/.

Greene, J. (2007). The Secret Joke of Kant's Soul. In W. Sinnott-Armstrong, ed., *Moral Psychology: The Neuroscience of Morality*, vol. 3. Cambridge, MA: MIT Press, 35–79.

Haidt, J. (2001). "The Emotional Dog and Its Rational Tail: A Social Intuitionist Approach to Moral Judgment." *Psychological Review*, 108 (4): 814–34.

Hare. R. M. (1981). *Moral Thinking*. Oxford: Oxford University Press.

Harman, G. (1977). *The Nature of Morality*. New York: Oxford University Press.

Hasan, A. & Fumerton, R. (2018). Foundationalist Theories of Epistemic Justification. In E. Zalta, ed., *The Stanford Encyclopedia of Philosophy* (Fall 2018 Edition), https://plato.stanford.edu/archives/fall2018/entries/justep-foundational/.

Haslanger, S. (2012). *Resisting Reality*. New York: Oxford University Press.

Hills, A. (2009). "Moral Testimony and Moral Epistemology." *Ethics*, 120(1): 94–127.

Hooker, B. (2000). *Ideal Code, Real World*. Oxford: Oxford University Press.

Hopkins, R. (2007). "What Is Wrong with Moral Testimony?" *Philosophy and Phenomenological Research*, 74(3): 611–34.

Horn, J. (2017). "Moral Realism, Fundamental Moral Disagreement, and Moral Reliability." *Journal of Value Inquiry*, 51(3): 363–81.

Huemer, M. (2005). *Ethical Intuitionism*. Houndmills, Basingstoke: Palgrave Macmillan.

(2007). "Compassionate Phenomenal Conservatism." *Philosophy and Phenomenological Research*, 74(1): 30–55.

(2008). "Revisionary Intuitionism." *Social Philosophy and Policy*, 25(1): 368–92.

Jackson, F.& Pettit, P. (1995). "Moral Functionalism and Moral Motivation." *Philosophical Quarterly*, 45(178): 20–40.

Johnston, M. (2001). "The Authority of Affect." *Philosophy and Phenomenological Research*, 63(1): 181–214.

Jones, K. (1999). "Second-Hand Moral Knowledge." *The Journal of Philosophy*, 96(2): 55–78.

(2006). Moral Epistemology. In F. Jackson & M. Smith, eds., *The Oxford Handbook of Contemporary Analytic Philosophy*. Oxford: Oxford University Press, 63–85.

Joyce, R. (2006). *The Evolution of Morality*. Cambridge, MA: Bradford.

Kagan, S. (1998). *Normative Ethics*. Boulder: Westview Press.

(2001). *Thinking About Cases*. In E. F. Paul, F. D. Miller, & J. Paul, eds., *Moral Knowledge*. Cambridge: Cambridge University Press.

Kahane, G. (2011). "Evolutionary Debunking Arguments." *Noûs*, 45(1): 103–25.

Kauppinen, A. (2018). Moral Sentimentalism. In E. Zalta, ed., *The Stanford Encyclopedia of Philosophy* (Winter 2018 Edition), https://plato.stanford.edu/archives/win2018/entries/moral-sentimentalism/.

Kim, B. (2017). "Pragmatic Encroachment in Epistemology." *Philosophy Compass*, 12(5).

Kelly, T. (2003). "Epistemic Rationality As Instrumental Rationality: A Critique." *Philosophy and Phenomenological Research*, 66(3): 612–40.

(2005). "Moorean Facts and Belief Revision, or Can the Skeptic Win?" *Philosophical Perspectives*, 19(1): 179–209.

Klein, P. (2015). Skepticism. In E. Zalta, ed., *The Stanford Encyclopedia of Philosophy* (Summer 2015 Edition) https://plato.stanford.edu/archives/sum2015/entries/skepticism/.

Korsgaard, C. (1996). *Sources of Normativity*. Cambridge: Cambridge University Press.

Lillehammer, H. (2007). *Companions in Guilt*. Houndmills, Basingstoke: Palgrave MacMillan.

Lutz, M.& Ross, J. (2018). Moral Skepticism. In T. McPherson and D. Plunkett, eds., *The Routledge Handbook of Metaethics*. New York: Routledge, 484–98.

Mackie, J. L. (1977). *Ethics: Inventing Right and Wrong*. Harmondsworth: Penguin.

Marx, K. & Engels, F. (1970). *The German Ideology*. W. Lough, trans., C. J. Arthur, ed. New York: International Publishers.

May, J. (2014). "Does Disgust Influence Moral Judgment?" *Australasian Journal of Philosophy*, 92 (1): 125–41.

McGrath, S. (2004). "Moral Knowledge by Perception." *Philosophical Perspectives*, 18(1): 209–28.

(2008). Moral Disagreement and Moral Expertise. In R. Shafer-Landau, ed., *Oxford Studies in Metaethics*, vol. 4. Oxford: Oxford University Press, 87–108.

(2011). "Skepticism about Moral Expertise As a Puzzle for Moral Realism." *Journal of Philosophy*, 108(3): 111–37.

McPherson, T. (2009). "Moorean Arguments and Moral Revisionism." *Journal of Ethics and Social Philosophy*, 3(1).

(2012). "Unifying Moral Methodology." *Pacific Philosophical Quarterly*, 93(4): 523–49.

(2015a). A Moorean Defense of the Omnivore? In B. Bramble & R. Fischer, *The Moral Complexities of Eating Meat*. Oxford: Oxford University Press, 118–34.

(2015b). The Methodological Irrelevance of Reflective Equilibrium. In C. Daly, ed., *The Palgrave Handbook of Philosophical Methods*. Houndmills, Basingstoke: Palgrave MacMillan, 652–74.

(2015c). Open Question Argument. In *Routledge Encyclopedia of Philosophy*, Taylor and Francis https://www.rep.routledge.com/articles/thematic/open-question-argument/v-1.

(2015d). "What Is at Stake in Debates among Normative Realists?" *Noûs*, 49 (1): 123–46.

(2018a). Authoritatively Normative Concepts. In R. Shafer-Landau, ed., *Oxford Studies in Metaethics*, vol. 13. Oxford: Oxford University Press, 253–77.

(2018b). Naturalistic Moral Realism, Moral Rationalism, and Non-Fundamental Epistemology. In K. Jones & F. Schroeter, eds., *The Many Moral Rationalisms*. Oxford: Oxford University Press, 187–209.

McPherson, T. & Plunkett, D. (2018). The Nature and Explanatory Ambitions of Metaethics. In T. McPherson & D. Plunkett, eds., *The Routledge Handbook of Metaethics*. New York: Routledge, 1–25.

(2020). Conceptual Ethics and the Methodology of Ethical Inquiry. In A. Burgess, H. Cappelan, & D. Plunkett, eds., *Conceptual Ethics and Conceptual Engineering*. Oxford: Oxford University Press, 274–303.

(Forthcoming). Evaluation Turned on Itself. In R. Shafer-Landau, ed., *Oxford Studies in Metaethics* vol. 16. Oxford: Oxford University Press.

Moore, G. E. (1903). "The Refutation of Idealism." *Mind*, 12(48): 433–53.

(1993 [1903]). *Principia Ethica*. T. Baldwin, ed. Cambridge: Cambridge University Press.

(1959). *Philosophical Papers*. London: George Allen & Unwin.

Nietzsche, F. (1966). *Beyond Good and Evil*. W. Kaufmann, trans. & ed. New York: Random House.

Olson, J. (2014). *Moral Error Theory: History, Critique, Defence*. New York: Oxford University Press.

Olsson, E. (2017). Coherentist Theories of Epistemic Justification. In E. Zalta, ed., *The Stanford Encyclopedia of Philosophy* (Spring 2017 Edition) https://plato.stanford.edu/archives/spr2017/entries/justep-coherence/.

Parfit, D. (1984). *Reasons and Persons*. Oxford: Oxford University Press.

Pollock, J. L. & Cruz, J. (1999) *Contemporary Theories of Knowledge*. Lanham, MD: Rowman and Littlefield.

Pritchard, D. Turri, J. & Carter, J. A. (2018). The Value of Knowledge. In E. Zalta, ed., *The Stanford Encyclopedia of Philosophy* (Spring 2018 Edition) https://plato.stanford.edu/archives/spr2018/entries/knowledge-value/.

Pryor, J. (2000). "The Skeptic and the Dogmatist." *Noûs* 34(4): 517–49.

Railton, P. (2003). *Facts, Values, and Norms.* Cambridge: Cambridge University Press.

Rawls, J. (1999a). The Independence of Moral Theory. In *Collected Papers*, S. Freeman, ed. Cambridge, MA: Harvard University Press, 286–302.

(1999b). *A Theory of Justice.* Rev. ed. Cambridge, MA: Belknap.

Rosen, G. (2018). Metaphysical Relations in Metaethics. In T. McPherson & D. Plunkett, eds., *The Routledge Handbook of Metaethics.* New York: Routledge, 151–69.

Ross, J. (2006). "Rejecting Ethical Deflationism." *Ethics* 116(4): 742–68.

Ross, W. D. (2002 [1930]). *The Right and the Good.* P. Stratton-Lake, ed. Oxford: Clarendon Press.

Royzman, E. B. Kim, K., & Leeman, R. F. (2015). "The Curious Tale of Julie and Mark: Unraveling the Moral Dumbfounding Effect." *Judgment and Decision Making*, 10(4): 296–313.

Russell, B. [Bertrand]. (2009 [1948]). *Human Knowledge.* New York: Routledge.

Russell, B. [Bruce]. (2017). A Priori Justification and Knowledge. In E. Zalta, ed., *The Stanford Encyclopedia of Philosophy* (Summer 2017 edition) https://plato.stanford.edu/archives/sum2017/entries/apriori/.

Rysiew, R. (2016). Epistemic Contextualism. In E. Zalta, ed., *The Stanford Encyclopedia of Philosophy* (Winter 2016 edition) https://plato.stanford.edu/archives/win2016/entries/contextualism-epistemology/.

Sampson, E. (2019). The Self-Undermining Arguments from Disagreement. In R. Shafer-Landau, ed., *Oxford Studies in Metaethics*, vol. 14. Oxford: Oxford University Press, 23–46.

Scanlon, T. M. (1998). *What We Owe to Each Other.* Cambridge, MA: Belknap.

Schechter, J. (2018). Explanatory Challenges in Metaethics. In T. McPherson & D. Plunkett, eds., *The Routledge Handbook of Metaethics.* New York: Routledge, 443–58.

Schroeder, M. (2010). *Non-Cognitivism in Ethics.* New York: Routledge.

Sepielli, A. (2019). Decision-Making Under Moral Uncertainty. In A. Zimmerman, K. Jones, & M. Timmons, eds., *The Routledge Handbook of Moral Epistemology.* New York: Routledge, 508–21.

Shafer-Landau, R. (2003). *Moral Realism: A Defence.* New York: Oxford University Press.

Shah, N. (2010). "The Limits of Normative Detachment." *Proceedings of the Aristotelian Society*, 110(3): 347–71.

Sidgwick, H. (1981 [1907]). *Methods of Ethics*, 7th ed. Indianapolis: Hackett.

Singer, S. (2005). "Ethics and Intuitions." *The Journal of Ethics*, 9(3/4): 331–52.

Sinnott-Armstrong, W. (2006). *Moral Skepticisms*. New York: OUP

(2008). Framing Moral Intuitions. In W. Sinnott-Armstrong, ed., *Moral Psychology*, vol. 2. *The Cognitive Science of Morality: Intuition and Diversity*. Cambridge, MA: MIT Press, 47–76.

(2011). An Empirical Challenge to Moral Intuitionism. In J. G. Hernandez, ed., *The New Intuitionism*. New York: Continuum, 11–28.

Sliwa, P. (2012). "In defense of Moral Testimony." *Philosophical Studies*, 158 (2): 175–95.

Smith, M. (1994). *The Moral Problem*. Oxford: Blackwell.

Smithies, D. (2019). *The Epistemic Role of Consciousness*. Oxford: Oxford University Press.

Star, D. (2008). "Moral Knowledge, Epistemic Externalism, and Intuitionism." *Ratio*, 21(3): 329–43.

Stojanovic, I. (2018). Metaethical Relativism. In T. McPherson & D. Plunkett, eds., *The Routledge Handbook of Metaethics*. New York: Routledge, 119–32.

Street, S. (2006). "A Darwinian Dilemma for Realist Theories of Value." *Philosophical Studies*, 127(1): 109–66.

(2008). "Reply to Copp: Naturalism, Normativity, and the Varieties of Realism Worth Worrying About." *Philosophical Issues*, 18(1): 207–28.

Thomson, J. J. (1985). "The Trolley Problem." *The Yale Law Journal*, 94(6): 1395–1415.

Tobin, T. W.& Jaggar, A. M. (2013). "Naturalizing Moral Justification: Rethinking the Method of Moral Epistemology." *Metaphilosophy*, 44(4): 409–39.

Turri, J., Alfano, M. & Greco, J. (2018). Virtue Epistemology. In E. Zalta, ed., *The Stanford Encyclopedia of Philosophy* (Summer 2018 Edition). https://plato.stanford.edu/archives/sum2018/entries/epistemology-virtue/.

Vavova, K. (2018). "Irrelevant Influences." *Philosophy and Phenomenological Research*, 96(1): 134–52.

Vayrynen, P. (2018). Doubts about Moral Perception. In A. Bergqvist & R. Cowan, eds., *Evaluative Perception*. Oxford: Oxford University Press, 109–28.

Wedgwood, R. (2014). Moral Disagreement among Philosophers. In M. Bergmann & P. Kain, eds., *Challenges to Moral and Religious Belief*. Oxford: Oxford University Press, 23–39.

Williamson, T. (2007). *The Philosophy of Philosophy*. Oxford: Oxford University Press.

Wolff, R. P. (1970). *In Defense of Anarchism*. New York: Harper & Row.

Zagzebski, L. (2012). *Epistemic Authority*. Oxford: Oxford University Press.

Zimmerman, A. (2010). *Moral Epistemology*. New York: Routledge.

Acknowledgements

I am grateful for valuable comments on drafts of this Element that were offered by Chris Cowie, Ben Eggleston, Jamie Fritz, Dale Miller, David Plunkett, Declan Smithies, and an anonymous referee for Cambridge University Press. As noted at the relevant locations in the text, parts of this Element draw on my previously published work, including:

McPherson, T. (2009), "Moorean Arguments and Moral Revisionism." *Journal of Ethics and Social Philosophy* 3(1): June 2009.

(2012), "Unifying Moral Methodology." *Pacific Philosophical Quarterly* 93 (4): December 2012.

(2015b), The Methodological Irrelevance of Reflective Equilibrium, in C. Daly, ed., *The Palgrave Handbook of Philosophical Methods.* (Palgrave, 2015).

(2018b), Naturalistic Moral Realism, Moral Rationalism, and Non-Fundamental Epistemology, in K. Jones & F. Schroeter, eds., *The Many Moral Rationalisms* (OUP, 2018).

McPherson, T. & Plunkett, D.(2018), The Nature and Explanatory Ambitions of Metaethics, *The Routledge Handbook of Metaethics.*

(forthcoming) *Conceptual Ethics and the Methodology of Ethical Inquiry.*

Section 5.2 draws significantly on unpublished work coauthored with David Plunkett.

Cambridge Elements ☰

Elements in Ethics

Ben Eggleston
University of Kansas

Ben Eggleston is a professor of philosophy at the University of Kansas. He is the editor of John Stuart Mill, *Utilitarianism: With Related Remarks from Mill's Other Writings* (Hackett, 2017) and a co-editor of *Moral Theory and Climate Change: Ethical Perspectives on a Warming Planet* (Routledge, 2020), *The Cambridge Companion to Utilitarianism* (Cambridge, 2014), and *John Stuart Mill and the Art of Life* (Oxford, 2011). He is also the author of numerous articles and book chapters on various topics in ethics.

Dale E. Miller
Old Dominion University, Virginia

Dale E. Miller is a professor of philosophy at Old Dominion University. He is the author of *John Stuart Mill: Moral, Social and Political Thought* (Polity, 2010) and a co-editor of *Moral Theory and Climate Change: Ethical Perspectives on a Warming Planet* (Routledge, 2020), *A Companion to Mill* (Blackwell, 2017), *The Cambridge Companion to Utilitarianism* (Cambridge, 2014), *John Stuart Mill and the Art of Life* (Oxford, 2011), and *Morality, Rules, and Consequences: A Critical Reader* (Edinburgh, 2000). He is also the editor-in-chief of *Utilitas*, and the author of numerous articles and book chapters on various topics in ethics broadly construed.

About the Series
This Elements series provides an extensive overview of major figures, theories, and concepts in the field of ethics. Each entry in the series acquaints students with the main aspects of its topic while articulating the author's distinctive viewpoint in a manner that will interest researchers.

Cambridge Elements ☰

Elements in Ethics

Elements in the Series

A full series listing is available at www.cambridge.org/EETH

Printed in the United States
By Bookmasters